Louise Hill Graham
Miriam Kleiner Young

Writing Power

Globe Book Company, Inc.

New York/Chicago/Cleveland

To
Elizabeth and Benjamin L. Hill
and
Dr. Howard D. Young

Louise Hill Graham is Assistant Principal, Supervision English, Walton High School, New York City.

Miriam Kleiner Young is Teacher of English and Communication Arts, Walton High School, New York City.

An Adaptation of "Playground is Alive With Running Water and Soaked Children" by Lisa Hammel from *The New York Times*, June 30, 1973, page 38, is reprinted by permission of The New York Times Company, Copyright © 1973.

Photo credits appear on page 156.

Edited by Julie DeWitt
Cover and Design by: Art Ritter
Photo Editor: Adelaide Garvin Ungerland
Cover Painting: Roy Lichtenstein. *Little Big Painting*. 1965. Oil on canvas. 68 x 80 inches.
Collection of Whitney Museum of American Art. Gift of the Friends of the Whitney Museum of American Art.

ISBN: 0-87065-285-0

Contents

INTRODUCTION
Getting Started

When you look at the empty box above, does it remind you of the blank sheets of composition paper you have stared at in the past? Do you often think you have nothing to write about? When you try to describe or explain something, do you write one or two sentences and then decide you have nothing more to say?

How about the box below? The picture inside it is called "The Three Musicians." Do you think that you could write more than two sentences about what you see in it?

There is probably much more to whatever you are looking at than you realize. One of the secrets of successful writing is the ability to look around and notice all the little things—the *details* that may seem so unimportant that you don't think they are worth mentioning.

There are many ways of looking at—and writing about—the world we live in. We can learn to describe the things we see by size, shape, color, or number. We can also talk about the way things feel, look, sound, taste, or smell. In just the same way, we all have a whole range of feelings and attitudes toward others, toward ourselves, and toward the things that are happening around us. We all feel different things—anger, love, hate, joy, boredom, pity—and we may all feel these things in different ways.

You are about to discover that writing can be an active and lively way of getting in touch with *your* special ideas and feelings. You will see that through writing, you can learn more about the kind of person you are and the kind of person you want to be, *and* you can have a good time doing it!

The skills you are about to learn will start you on your way.

1

Seeing the Details

What's wrong with this picture?

There are at least eight things wrong with it. Study it carefully to see how many you can find. Make a list of all the mistakes you spot.

Turn to page 15 to see how sharp you were. How many wrong details did you find? Four? Six? All eight? Wonderful! You see, you *can* find details when you look for them. How did you do it? You went back again and again if you had to, examining the picture more and more closely until you found everything. This is just the kind of searching we have to do if we are to have something to write about. Looking is not enough. We have to **see** when we look.

How often, though, do we look at things, or places, or people right next to us without really seeing them?

Think about the following questions. See how fast you can come up with the answers about these things you do and see every day.

1. On what side of the sink is the hot-water tap?
2. Are the buttons sewn on the left or right side of a shirt front?
3. Is the button side the same for men's shirts and for women's shirts?
4. Which arm do you put through your sleeve first?
5. Which leg do you start with when you put on your pants?
6. Which shoe do you put on first?
7. Which way do you turn the knob to open your classroom door?
8. On a traffic light, is the red at the top or at the bottom?

Could you answer each one? Did everyone in your class agree on the same answers? If not, it may be that you don't really see as many details in the world around you as you think you do. Remember, the harder you look, the more you see. The more you see, the better you write.

What's happening in this picture?

There are many different things all going on at once in this picture. See how many you can find. How many people are there in the picture? What are they doing? Make a list of all the things you see.

Now turn to page 28 and check to see how many details you were able to find. If you missed one, look at the picture again and try to figure out why you didn't see it. Were you more interested in something else that was going on? Did you think this one detail wasn't very important? Did you look at the picture long enough and hard enough and often enough?

If you found all the details, congratulations! You certainly have a very sharp eye!

Trying It on Your Own

1. Without turning around to look, write a missing-person's description of the student sitting behind you. Height? Weight? Color of hair? Color of eyes? Does he or she wear eyeglasses? What kind of clothing is this student wearing today? What colors? Any special features or identifying marks?

2. A television reporter wants to interview you on TV as a "typical" student on a "typical" school day. The reporter wants to know everything you did today, and everyone you saw or spoke to, since you arrived in school this morning. To prepare yourself, write down every single thing you've seen or done today until now.

3. You are the only witness to an automobile accident. Fortunately, no one is hurt, but both cars have been badly damaged. Write an accident report for the insurance company, telling *exactly* what happened. What time did the accident happen? Was the road wet or icy? Did the drivers obey the traffic signals? In which direction was each car traveling? What did each driver do? In what order did these things happen to them?

2

Using All Your Senses

Think about a long piece of chalk. What can you say about it? After noting that it is white, and long and slim in shape, what other details can you find?

You can say that it feels hard and smooth in your fingers. How about the way it sounds when it scratches on the board or the snap you hear when you break it in two? How about the fine, filmy dust that settles on your fingers or clothes as you use it to write on the board? Does chalk have an odor? Does it have a taste? You see, there is a lot to say about a piece of chalk, or about almost anything else for that matter.

2-1 Skill Builder: Recognizing Sensory Details

How would you answer the following questions? Write at least two words or phrases about each thing.

1. What does an old piece of bread taste like?

2. What does a sheet that's just come out of the laundry smell like?

3. What does the siren sound like when an ambulance is racing down the street?

4. What does a snowball feel like when you're shaping it in your hands?

5. What does a forkful of spaghetti look like as you bring it to your mouth?

2-2 SKILL BUILDER: CHECKING OUT A REAL LIVE APPLE!

Bring an apple to school with you tomorrow. Don't give it to the teacher! Look at it closely. Then answer all of the following questions.

1. What color is it? Is it only one color? What other colors, or specks of color, do you see?

2. What other things identify the look of this particular apple? Dark spots? Holes? Lines? Any bumps on it? What kind? How many?

3. What shape is the apple? Is it really round? Look again.

4. Feel the skin of the apple. What does it feel like?

5. Lift the apple in your hand. Try to guess how heavy it is. What else can you think of that feels as heavy or as light as the apple?

6. Smell the apple. Where is the smell strongest, at the stem or on the sides? What does it smell like?

7. Now, bite into it. What sounds do you hear as you sink your teeth into the apple? What sounds do you hear as you chew it?

8. What does the apple taste like? What does the taste remind you of?

You know about all these things because you have **five senses** that give you the information. With these senses, you are able to **see, hear, taste, smell,** and **touch** things in the world around you. Every time you write down the things you can see, hear, taste, smell, or touch, you are using **sensory details**. These are the details that bring your writing to life.

9

Suppose you had to describe a luscious, chocolate-covered cherry.

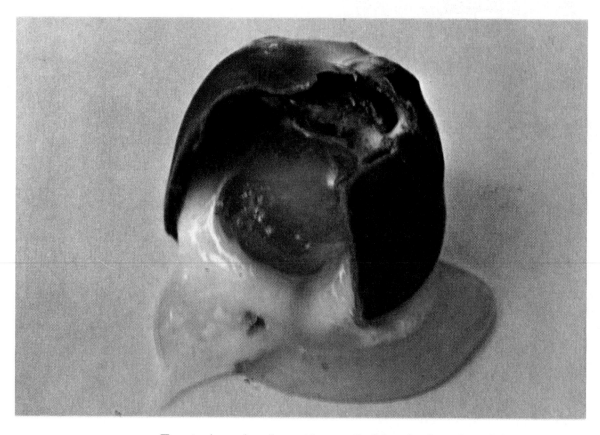

Try to imagine how the real thing looks: the rich red of the cherry in the center, the milky-white of the syrup flowing around it, the shiny, dark-brown chocolate coating. Think about how it tastes: the soft, creamy syrup sliding down your throat, the sticky sweetness of the cherry as it gives way under your teeth, the warmth of the smooth chocolate on your tongue. Feel the chocolate melting and oozing between your fingers. Sniff the rich, fruity smell. What kind of sound would you make as you slowly sucked out the syrup and saved the chocolate for last?

Can you see how writing down all these sensory details would make the candy seem real enough to eat? Can you see that the more you can say about the way things taste, smell, sound, feel, and look, the more interesting your writing will be?

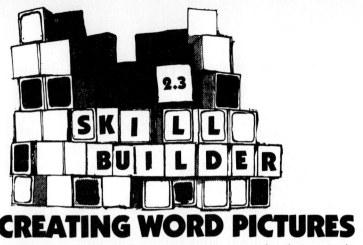

CREATING WORD PICTURES

There are many things you come across every day that appeal to your five senses. Let's see what kinds of sensory details you have noticed about them.

    A.   Here are some things you often see:
        1. flowers 2. trucks 3. bicycles

Write a phrase or sentence that creates a "picture" of each thing for your reader. (A sample is done for you below.)

Sample: School Jacket — bright and shiny, grass-green jacket with golden racing stripes circling one arm and brass buttons glinting in the sun

    B.   Here are some things you often taste or smell: (These two senses are often almost the same.)
        1. soda 2. pizza 3. fresh-cut lemon

Write a phrase or sentence for each one that will make your reader recognize the taste or smell. (A sample is done for you below.)

Sample: Egg Roll — crispy, flaky shell wrapped around chewy, fresh-diced, spicy vegetables

    C.   Here are some things you often touch:
        1. kittens 2. marshmallows 3. brick wall

Write a phrase or sentence for each one that tells your reader how it feels when you touch it. (A sample is done for you below.)

Sample: Winter-Scarf — rough, scratchy, itchy wool rubbing against the back of your neck

    D.   Here are some things you often hear:
        1. subway trains or railroad trains 2. exploding firecrackers 3. potato chips

Write a phrase or sentence for each one that will make your reader "hear" the sound. (A sample is done for you below.)

Sample: Chicken Frying — sizzling, hissing oil spitting angrily against the pan

BUILDING UP YOUR WORD POWER: SENSORY WORDS

Did you get stuck in describing any of the things on the lists? Did you have trouble with the potato chips, for instance? After you said they sounded crispy or they snapped in your hand, did you run out of words?

These are some of the things you might have said:

they <u>rustle</u> together in their thin cellophane bag
they <u>crumble</u> in your fingers
they <u>crunch</u> against your teeth

These kinds of words are called **sensory words**. They add life and sparkle to what you say. They make your writing more vivid and exciting.

2-4 SKILL BUILDER: USING SENSORY WORDS

Here are some other sensory words. Study them, and then go back to the exercise you just finished. See how many of these new words you can now add to make your phrases and sentences even more alive. This time, you can choose any of the sensory words for any of the things you are writing about.

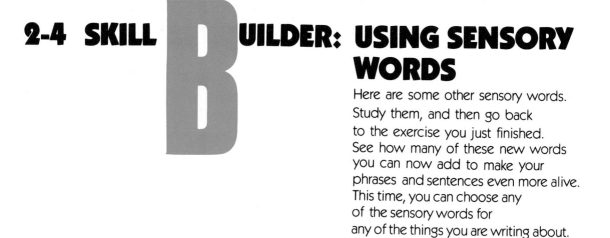

1. **mouth-watering:** so delicious that it makes you hungry
2. **thundering:** sounding like the booming noise of thunder
3. **screeching:** high-pitched, almost screaming
4. **ear-splitting:** so loud that it seems to hurt the ears
5. **crimson:** a clear, deep red
6. **tangy:** sharp and spicy
7. **fluffy:** soft, puffed out
8. **crusty:** having a hard, crispy edge
9. **crackling:** a snapping sound (like the sound you hear when you pour milk on dry cereal)
10. **glistening:** shining (like water in sunlight)
11. **tingling:** a tickling feeling in the mouth or nose

Trying It on Your Own

1. Look at this picture of a baseball game. Can't you just see the dust, hear the noise, and smell the franks and fries that are being sold in the stands?

   Write your own description of everything you would see, hear, taste, smell, and touch if you were actually at this game.

2. Here is a menu you might see in a restaurant. On the left are the names of the foods the restaurant serves. Copy the names. Next to each one, write a description of the food. Write it so full of sensory details that customers would want to order that food. (The first one has been done for you.)

MENU

Corn on the Cob	Golden yellow kernels of fresh, juicy corn dripping with sweet, melted butter.
Green salad	
Cheeseburger	
Hot Dog	
French Fried Potatoes	
Ice Cream	
Milkshake	
Chocolate Cake	

3. In this picture, you get an idea of the excitement of a disco—the lights, the sounds, the movement.

Imagine that a new disco has opened up in town. Write a television commercial so full of the sights and sounds (and any other sensory details) of a disco that people would want to pay the price of admission. Remember—you are trying to *sell* the attractions of the disco—so build up those sensory details!

Answers to the Puzzle Picture on Page 4
1. woman with hands for feet
2. three-legged dog
3. man upsidedown
4. hydrant with lightbulb and plug
5. woman sideways in window
6. bicycle with no seat
7. house number upside down
8. door hinges at top of door rather than side

3

Dealing with Feeling

What feelings are expressed in this picture?

The picture shows a person who is suffering. We know this because of the details the artist has given us.

1. The person is clutching his head between his hands as if he is in pain.
2. The mouth is open as if the person is screaming.
3. The eyes are wide and staring as if the person is seeing something terrible.
4. The person looks more like a skeleton than a human being—as if the person is starving.

There are other important details, too. We might not spot them right away, but they are there.

1. This person is all alone on a bridge. The only other people in the picture are walking away. It is as though no one in the world cares.
2. The picture is dark and full of heavy black lines.
3. Even the sky looks stormy and threatening.

3-1 SKILL BUILDER: RECOGNIZING EMOTIONAL DETAILS

Look at this next picture. How do you think *these* people are feeling? What is it in the picture that makes you think they are feeling this way? What do their faces say? How about their hands; the way they are sitting, the things on the table?

List as many details as you can that make you think they are feeling a certain way.

When you talk over these pictures in class, you may discover that the way you saw them was different from the way some of your classmates saw them. For example, some may have thought that the two people in the first picture were walking toward the screaming man, not walking away. That is because, very often, there is more than one way of seeing or understanding the same thing.

Take a good look at the following examples:

Are the stairs going up or down?	Is this a vase or two people looking at each other?	Is this an old woman or a young girl?
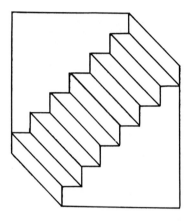		

Whichever you saw, you were right. Your eyes can shift up and down, back and forth, left and right, putting the same thing together in different ways.

Look at the picture on page 20 for 15 seconds. As you look at it, try to notice how you're looking, in which direction your eyes are moving, in which order you are seeing things.

1. What is the first thing you saw?
2. What is the second?
3. Did you look at the whole picture or at separate parts of it in turn?
4. Which way are the birds flying?
5. How many birds are there?
6. List everything you see in the lower left corner of the picture.

Did you notice that everything on the left side of the picture is the exact opposite of everything on the right side? If you said the birds were flying to the right, you were talking about the white birds. If you said they were flying to the left, you meant the black ones. Again, whichever you said, you were right. Whether you saw the white or the black parts of the picture—which were really the same things—depended on how you looked at it.

Sometimes our feelings are that way, too. Sometimes we look at the bright side of things. Other times, we look at the dark side of things. Sometimes what looks good to us looks bad to others.

That is because the way we feel is influenced by the way we think about things. Each of us tends to concentrate on what is most important to us. This is one big reason why writing can be an adventure. There are so many possible reactions to the very same situation—or even to the very same word.

A reaction is the way we feel about something. Usually, we don't have to think about it. Certain words, or certain situations, are like triggers for us. We know how we will feel when we see them or hear them.

SKILL BUILDER

REACTING TO "LOADED" WORDS

Here is a list of some strong reaction words. Number 1 to 10 on a sheet of paper. Read the first word quickly. Next to number 1, write down the very first thing that comes to your mind. Then do the same for words 2, 3, and so on. Do not look back. Do not change anything you write. There are no right or wrong answers.

1. mother	6. time
2. school	7. loneliness
3. fear	8. police
4. money	9. fire
5. hate	10. friend

You didn't have any trouble reacting to any one of the words on the list, did you? That's because you probably have strong feelings about many of them. Compare your answers to the ones your classmates wrote. How many answers are the same? Which ones are different? Talk over the different feelings that each student's answers show. People have these different reactions because their experiences are different. Any reaction, however, is right if it's true for you.

If your class had the topic "A Rainy Day" to write about, for example, one student might talk about how boring it is to be cooped up in the house. Another student might write about how happy he is that the pouring rain is washing his car so he won't have to do it himself. Someone else might be furious that a big play-off game is being rained out. Whatever you say about that rainy day is okay because that's how YOU feel about it.

BUILDING UP YOUR WORD POWER: GETTING RID OF TIRED WORDS

Sometimes it's hard to say exactly how you *do* feel because you don't have the right word. Other times, all you can think of are tired old words like "mad," "glad," "sad," and "bad." Words like these have been used so often that they've lost their power. There are other words you can use that will really get your meaning across. Some of them are on the following list.

Which word you use depends on how strong your feeling is. For example, you might say you're "scared" of failing a test. That's not the same kind of fear you would feel riding in a speeding car whose brakes were gone. You might be "scared" of failing, but you'd be "terrified" of dying! There's a world of difference between the two kinds of fear, isn't there? The same is true for all the other feeling words.

3-3
SKILL BUILDER: MATCHING WORDS TO FEELINGS

Check out the <u>exact</u> meaning of each word in the chart. What can you learn about the words that follow the "tired" words listed in the first column?

BAD	sorry	regretful	upset	anguished
SAD	unhappy	dejected	miserable	heartbroken
GLAD	pleased	delighted	thrilled	overjoyed
MAD	irritated	angry	furious	enraged
SCARED	nervous	alarmed	fearful	terrified

Now tell which word from any other column on the chart would match your feelings if you were in the situations described below.

1.

Someone you like *very* much has started to notice you and compliments you on the way you look. *How would you feel? How would you feel if this person invited you to a party?*

2.

You're standing in a school cafeteria line, hungry, and waiting your turn. Someone pushes right in front of you and gets the piece of the cake that you wanted. *How would you feel? How would you feel if this person were a good friend of yours?*

3.

You lost your temper and said terrible things to someone who has always been very kind to you. *How would you feel? How would you feel if this person died before you got the chance to say you were sorry?*

4.

You're riding home on the subway late at night. Suddenly, you realize you're the only person left on the train. *How would you feel? How would you feel if a tough-looking man suddenly got on the train?*

5.

You've practiced hours every day for a year to make the team. Now, at the tryouts, you realize that you're not good enough. *How would you feel? How would you feel if you learned that this was the last time you could ever try out for that team?*

6.

You leave your new bicycle chained outside a store. When you come out, you discover that the bicycle has been stolen. *How would you feel? How would you feel if you had borrowed the bike from your best friend?*

Trying It on Your Own

1. Here are three situations about which each of us might feel differently. Some of us might love to find ourselves in one or another of them. Some of us might hate them all.

   a. Being made the teacher's pet
   b. Being interviewed on a television news program
   c. Being invited to a very fancy party to which none of your friends has been invited.

   Choose the one you have the strongest feelings about—either love or hate. Write down all the good—or bad—feelings you would have about the situation you choose. Try to use some of the words from the list on page 22 to help you put across your feelings.

2. You have just found out that your best friend told your most personal secrets to someone else. Write down *all* the feelings you would have at this moment. See if you can use any of the words on the list on page 22.

3. Sometimes you can have mixed feelings about something. Suppose your dog is very sick and is in terrible pain. Write down *all* the feelings you would have when the animal doctor says the dog must be destroyed. You don't want to lose your dog, but you don't want it to continue suffering either. Are there any words listed on page 22 that can help you tell how you would really feel?

4 Putting It All Together

In the last three chapters, you have been practicing three very important skills which can help to make your writing interesting and lively.

1. recognizing details
2. using sensory words
3. expressing feelings

The picture on page 26 gives you a chance to put them all together. Study it carefully.

You may think you are seeing things from inside the cabin. Others in your class may think they are looking at the scene from the outside. You and your classmates may also have different feelings about the picture. However, there are certain details that everyone will agree on. Think about the following questions:

1. What are the walls made of? How would they feel if you touched them?
2. Notice the wooden posts on each side of the door. What condition is the wood in? What might stick in your hand if you ran your fingers over this kind of wood?
3. What is the floor made of? What do the floor, the walls, and the logs on either side of the doorway tell you about the kind of building this might be?
4. What is standing on the floor to the left of the door? How would you describe its size and shape?

5. How many boxes do you see on the floor all the way over on the right hand side of the picture? What's inside the top one? Can you tell if there is anything inside the bottom one?
6. What do you see on the other side of the door? Is the door half-open or half-closed? (Note that this is the one thing on this list you *can't* be sure of.)

After you have looked carefully at all these details and talked them over in class, copy the following paragraph in your notebook. Fill in the blank spaces with words or phrases that most clearly describe these details and the way you feel about them. Try to make your paragraph so real that someone who has never seen this picture would know just what it looks like and just what feelings it gives you. See if you can use any of the sensory words you learned in Chapter Two or any of the feeling words you learned in Chapter Three to help you say what you really mean.

This is a picture of a deserted log cabin. The walls are made of _____. It looks as though the people who lived here _____.
The large green door most probably makes a _____ sound when you open or close it completely. On the floor near the door is a _____. It is crumpled and _____. Folding the bag so it looks like this would make a _____ sound. The wooden post behind the bag has started to _____. If you ran your hand over it, this wooden post would probably feel _____ and _____. Chances are the room smells _____. The darkness beyond the door makes me feel _____. I feel this way because _____

_____.

Answers to the "What's Happening" Picture in Chapter 1, Page 6

1. You should be able to count at least 35 people in this picture. There are really 53!

2. Beneath the window, an old woman is begging.

3. In the middle of the picture, 11 people are moving through a tunnel toward the white platform. You should be able to count at least nine of them.

4. In the middle of the platform, there are two soldiers on horseback. One of the horses is rearing up on its hind legs.

5. To the left on the platform, there is a group of soldiers wearing helmets, watching the rearing horse. Can you find 17 of these soldiers? (One of them is half-hidden behind the horse, but if you look closely, you will see the soldier's legs.) You should be able to count at least 10.

6. Two figures on the ground are scrambling to get away from the other horse.

7. On the right side of the white platform, there are 13 more people. Some are simply watching the action in the middle, others stand with arms outstretched. You should be able to pick out almost all 13.

8. In the lower left corner of the picture, an animal searches for food among the ruins.

9. At the bottom of the picture, below the huge green jack-in-the-box, two men are talking.

5
Opening Up the Details

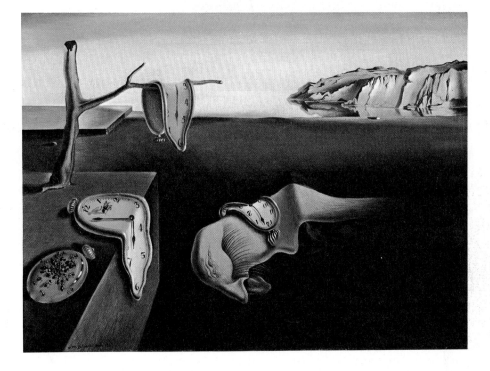

It would be hard to describe this painting to a friend who had not seen it, wouldn't it? If you said it was a picture of some strange-looking watches, you would be telling an important detail. If you said something about the bare tree and the rocky cliff, you would be using good sensory words to describe the tree and the cliff. If you also said that the picture seems strange and scary, you would be dealing with feeling.

Everything you said would be right on target. But would your friend really know exactly what the picture is like? Your honest answer would have to be "no." The problem is that you just haven't told enough. For your friend to get the true picture, you would have to explain why the watches are so strange-looking. You would have to tell how the tree and the cliff really look. You would also have to say what makes the picture so scary and strange.

To get across what we really mean to say, we have to **open up the details**. That means that we have to give more information about everything. We have to tell more about what is in the picture. We have to say more about how the things in the picture look or taste, sound or feel. We have to tell more about why the picture makes us feel a certain way. Just making one statement about each of these things is not enough to tell it as it really is.

This is true of everything that we write. We have to weave things together—the details, the senses, the feelings. We have to write more than one line about each of them. We have to build sentence by sentence, adding more sensory details or explaining more about why we feel the way we do. We have to open up the details.

The trick is to ask yourself three key questions about each sentence that you write:

1. What else can I add to these details?
2. What other sensory words can I use?
3. What more can I say about my feelings?

You need to do this kind of opening up for all your writing to make your ideas clear and sharp. Copping out with the excuse, "Oh, you know what I mean!" isn't fair to yourself or to your reader. You *can* tell more about what, how, and why. You can open up the details and say exactly what you mean.

You do this all the time, without even thinking about it, when you're talking to someone. That's because you can tell by the other person's face or by the questions that he or she asks that your message isn't clear. When you don't make things clear, you can end up with some pretty funny misunderstandings. The following exercises may show you how things can go wrong.

5-1 SKILL BUILDER: GIVING DIRECTIONS

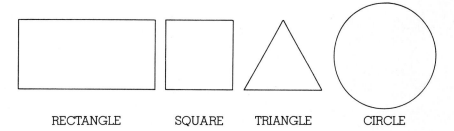

RECTANGLE   SQUARE   TRIANGLE   CIRCLE

You know what all these figures are. Look them over again. On your paper, arrange these shapes any way you like. You may use any of them more than once, but don't have more than seven figures in your finished drawing. Below is a sample of what you might draw. Don't use this one, though. Make up your own arrangement.

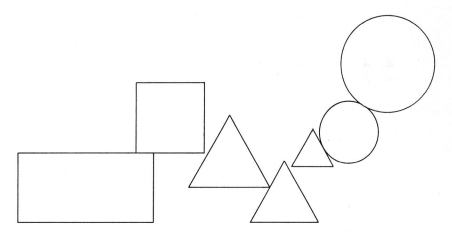

When everyone's sketch is done, choose a partner. Don't let your partner see what you have drawn. Give directions to your partner in such a way that he or she can draw your design exactly, without seeing it.

You must not look at what your partner is putting down on paper either. Your job is just to give directions. Your partner's job is just to draw what you tell him or her to put down on paper.

Does the picture your partner drew according to your directions look just like yours? If not, you probably didn't explain enough, tell enough, or describe enough! In other words, you didn't open up the details. Now you can see that just saying, "You know what I mean!" does not work.

Now, choose a different partner. This time, watch what your partner is doing as you give the directions. If you see that your partner is not doing it right, help, as much as you can.

Tell your partner things like

A. Start drawing the shapes at a certain part of the paper.

B. Go higher or lower.

C. Move the shape to the right or the left.

D. Make the shape larger or smaller.

This second sketch probably turned out much better than the first. Giving more details—**opening them up**—is what made the difference.

That's why you need to ask yourself these questions again for every one of the sentences that you write:

1. What else can I add to these details?
2. What other sensory words can I use?
3. What more can I say about my feelings?

MOVING FROM THE GENERAL TO THE SPECIFIC

For each sentence below, follow the instructions given in the parentheses. Try to add at least two extra sentences of your own to the sentence you are given.

1. There's always a lot of action on my street. *(Tell what the children are doing. Tell what the grown-ups are doing. Tell what kind of traffic is going by.)*

2. Sometimes in one day, I go from one mood to another. *(Tell what different feelings, or moods, you have during a single day.)*

3. Spaghetti is a fun food to eat. *(Tell what the spaghetti looks and tastes like. Tell why it's hard to get it from your plate to your mouth.)*

4. I can't talk to my parents. *(Tell why you feel this way.)*

5. The sky at sunset is beautiful. *(Tell what the sky looks like. Tell what colors you see in the sky.)*

6. You can always tell when people are nervous. *(Tell what kinds of things people do that show they feel nervous.)*

7. A puppy in a pet shop is cute. *(Tell what the puppy looks like. Tell all the things it does that make it cute.)*

8. I hate to get out of bed on a cold winter morning. *(Tell how it feels to be under the covers. Tell what it's like when you get out of the bed.)*

9. Many people love to gamble. *(Tell what things people bet on. Tell why some people love to gamble.)*

10. I love disco dancing. *(Tell which dances you love. Tell how you feel when you're dancing.)*

Trying It on Your Own

Here's a game called *uppers and downers*. Completing a sentence with pleasant details makes an upper. Completing it with unpleasant details makes a downer.

This is a sample of the way it works:

Shopping in a supermarket can be a real upper when the store is sparkling clean and everything you need is on sale and they're giving out free samples and the checkout clerk gets you out in ten minutes flat.

Shopping in a supermarket can be a real downer when you have only three items to pay for and the express line is closed and the woman in front of you has a cart loaded with groceries and a handful of coupons to be counted out.

Now you play the game. On a separate sheet of paper, complete each of the following uppers and downers with as many pleasant or unpleasant details as you can think of.

1. Getting an offer of a summer job can be a real upper

   when _____.

   Getting an offer of a summer job can be a real downer

   when _____.

2. Being the tallest one in the class can be a real upper

   when _____.

   Being the tallest one in the class can be a real downer

   when _____.

3. Having a picnic on a summer day can be a real upper

   when _____.

   Having a picnic on a summer day can be a real downer

   when _____.

6

Telling What, Why, and How

Look again at the picture on page 29. Here's the kind of paragraph that might be written about it where the details are not opened up:

This is a weird picture. The watches are funny-looking. The tree and the beach make everything look lonely and scary. It's like something you would see in a nightmare.

This paragraph is a lot like the sketch your first partner made of your drawing back on page 31. The pieces are there, but they don't add up to the complete picture. We don't know **what** is weird-looking. We don't know **why** the watches are funny-looking. We don't know **how** the tree and the beach make everything look lonely and scary. Let's take it line by line to see how we can open it up.

6-1 SKILL BUILDER: TELLING MORE ABOUT WHAT, WHY, AND HOW

1. *Start with the first sentence.* This is a weird picture.

2. *Why does the picture seem weird?* <u>The watches are funny-looking.</u>

3. *What is funny-looking about the watches? Use sensory words to describe them.* <u>They are soft and long. Some are stretched out of shape.</u>

   What do they look like? <u>They look like clothes hung out to dry. One watch is covered with black bugs.</u>

4. *Add the next sentence.* <u>The tree and the beach make everything look lonely and scary.</u>

5. *How do the tree and the beach make things look lonely and scary? Use sensory words to describe the tree and the beach.* <u>The tree is dead and has no leaves. A long, thin watch is stretched over one branch like a wet blanket. The beach is empty, except for a strange sea-monster asleep on the sand.</u>

   Why does the picture make you feel lonely and scared? <u>There are no people anywhere. It's dark and deserted. Nothing looks the way it's supposed to look.</u>

6. *End with the last sentence.* <u>It's like something you would see in a nightmare.</u>

If we add the new sentences we've written to the ones we started out with, we come up with a brand-new paragraph that looks like this:

This is a weird picture. The watches are funny-looking. They are soft and long. Some are stretched out of shape. They look like clothes hung out to dry. One watch is covered with black bugs. The tree and the beach make everything look lonely and scary. The tree is dead and has no leaves. A long, thin watch is stretched over one branch like a wet blanket. The beach is empty, except for a strange sea-monster asleep on the sand. There are no people anywhere. It's dark and deserted. Nothing looks the way it's supposed to look. It's like something you would see in a nightmare.

You can see that this new paragraph is a lot better than the first one. Anyone who reads it would surely get a better idea of what the picture on page 29 is all about. Any reader would also get a clearer understanding of just how you feel about it.

Now that you see how it can be done, look at the circus picture on this page. Remember all the fun and excitement of a visit to a real circus? Wouldn't it be boring just to write that the circus is great, or that you had a terrific time at the circus? Wouldn't it be a lot better to open up the details so your reader can share all that fun and excitement with you?

Close your eyes and think about the lights, the colors, the costumes. What do you see at a circus? What do you smell? What do you hear? How do you feel when you watch the brave lion tamers, the daring trapeze artists, the funny clowns?

6-2 SKILL BUILDER: ADDING LIVELY DETAILS

Let's see what kinds of details you could open up about the circus. On the left is a list of some possible details you might want to write about. On the right are some ideas for opening them up. For each of the details, try to write at least two sentences that follow the directions on the right.

1. When I'm watching a three-ring circus, I don't know what to look at first.	What do you see in each ring? Don't just name the acts; tell what is going on in each ring.
2. I hold my breath when the lion tamer cracks a whip at the roaring lions.	Why do you hold your breath? Name the feelings you have. Describe what goes through your mind at this exciting moment.
3. The clowns come tumbling in, making everybody laugh.	What do the clowns look like? Describe what they do that's so funny.
4. Even the food at the circus tastes great.	How do the hot dogs look and smell? How does the cotton candy look, feel, and taste? How do the peanuts and popcorn sound when you eat them?
5. What I love best of all are the fantastic costumes.	What are the costumes like? Describe the colors, imagine the feel of the furs and the feathers. How do the costumes look in the bright spotlight?

You might want to combine everything you've written about the circus into one big paragraph like the one on page 36. Start with the first detail given on the left side of this page. Then add the sentences you wrote to open up that detail. Next, write the second detail given on the left. Add your own sentences to that one, and so one.

Did you think that you couldn't write a paragraph as long and full as this one? Now you can—if you **open up the details.**

Trying It on Your Own

Answer each question below, and include as many details about **what, why,** and **how** as you can. Write your answers in your notebook.

Tell **what** you would be.
Tell **how** you would look or sound.
Tell **why** you chose your particular answer.

SAMPLE: If you were a tree, what kind of tree would you be?

ANSWER: I'd be a king-sized Christmas tree with twinkling lights all over my shiny green branches and heaps of presents underneath me because I love to make people happy.

1. If you were an animal, what animal would you be?

2. If you were a season of the year, what season would you be?

3. If you were a famous person in history, what person would you be?

4. If you were a song, what song would you be?

5. If you were a bird, what bird would you be?

6. If you were a pair of shoes, what kind of shoes would you be?

7
Grouping Action Details

Another way of opening details is to put together—or to **group**—similar things, like **action words**. For example, if you wanted to tell what happened at a movie when the film broke, you might write:

The audience got angry.

But if you wanted to open up the details so that your reader would know just how angry the audience really got, you might add sentences like these:

The audience booed. People whistled. Some stamped their feet. Others shouted and yelled.

Action words like these—boo, shout, whistle, yell, stamp—are all related to the situation given in the first sentence. They can all be used to tell more about that situation. By telling more with action words, you open up the details.

Here's another example. Suppose you were writing about the way you might feel if you were face to face with animals like the ones on the next page.

You might start out with a line like this:

I'd get scared if I saw snarling wild dogs.

You could open it up by adding:

My hands would start to <u>shake</u>. My heart would <u>pound</u> against my ribs. My knees would <u>knock</u> together. I'd <u>jump</u> back as fast as I could. I'd <u>race</u> away in the opposite direction.

You can see that all the underlined words tell more about your fear. They open up the details, and make that fear real.

RECOGNIZING VIVID VERBS

Good action words, called verbs, always make your writing more vivid and exciting. A line like, "The runners ran a great race" doesn't tell your reader much does it? Think how much stronger it would be if you added sentences like these:

The runners sprinted forward at the sound of the gun.
They thundered down the track.
They leaped over the hurdles.
They crashed through the tape at the finish line.
They panted for air at the end of the race.

The action words make a big difference, don't they? There are many other words like these that you can use. Let's look at just a few of these lively action words.

BUILDING UP YOUR WORD POWER: ACTION WORDS

A. Here are some action words—and their meanings—that might help you to open up the details if you were writing about a CROWD.

1. **hasten:** to hurry
2. **scurry:** to run in all directions
3. **jostle:** to push or shove lightly
4. **collide with:** to bump into

B. Here are some action words—and their meanings—that might help you to open up the details if you were writing about a CRANKY PERSON.

1. **whine:** to demand things in a crybaby voice
2. **pout:** to push out one's lips in a show of anger
3. **sulk:** to show anger by refusing to speak to anybody
4. **complain:** to find fault with your own life or with the things other people do

C. Here are some action words—and their meanings—that might help you to open up the details if you were writing about DANCING.

1. **whirl:** to turn rapidly around and around
2. **glide:** to move smoothly and continuously, like a skater across the ice
3. **swivel:** to turn around quickly
4. **soar:** to rise high in the air

7-1 SKILL BUILDER:
CHOOSING THE BEST ACTION WORD

Study the above words and their meanings. Then, copy the following sentences on a sheet of your notebook paper. For each sentence, write the new word that you think fits in best.

1. When my sister gets angry, she goes off alone to her room to _____ .

2. In the fall, the wind makes the leaves _____ through the air.

3. I saw the black car _____ the blue car when they both went through the red light.

4. I watched the airplane _____ off the runway into the sky.

5. The candy store owner told the kids not to _____ around on the shaky counter stools.

6. When people _____ me in a line, I get annoyed.

7. Children who _____ for everything they want should not get their way.

8. The sea was so calm that the boat could _____ right through the water.

9. The sudden rain made people _____ for shelter.

10. People who _____ look like babies about to cry.

11. After he overslept, he had to _____ through breakfast to get out of the house on time.

12. Old people often _____ that no one pays any attention to them.

Now that you've practiced using these action words, here are four more sentences for you to think about. They will give you a chance to use the words again, this time any way you like:

1. Bumper cars are one of the best rides of all.
2. Spoiled brats always give me a pain.
3. The action at a hockey game can be fast and furious.
4. Rude people are the first to show they're insulted when others are rude to them.

7-2 SKILL BUILDER: ADDING ACTION DETAILS

For each of the four sentences above, do the following:

a. Copy the sentence in your notebook.

b. Check back to page 42 to see again how action words can open up the details.

c. Then, add as many more sentences as you can. Use all the action words that fit. Note that you may use the same action words in different sentence groupings.

Trying It on Your Own

Below is a series of newspaper headlines. Open up the details by answering, as fully as you can, the questions below each one. Feel free to add any other details you can think of on your own.

Remember to keep asking yourself the three key questions:

1. What else can I add to these details?
2. What other sensory words can I use?
3. What more can I say about feelings?

Try to use some—or all—of those action words on page 42.

HOME TEAM LOSES HEARTBREAKER

What happened? What was the final score? How many batters did the pitcher strike out? Did he stay in the game all the way? Did an outfielder make—or miss—a super catch? What made the loss of this particular game so sad? Who was especially heartbroken about it?

TEACHER QUITS AFTER ONE DAY AT SCHOOL

Tell everything the students did in class to upset the new teacher. Tell how it got started. How did everyone get involved? How did the classroom sound while all this was going on? How did the room look when it was all over?

FOODS OF ALL NATIONS SOLD AT STREET FAIR

What foods were sold? How did they smell? taste? look? What sounds could be heard at the fair? How many people were there? What did the people look like? sound like? What did they do at the fair?

8

Building Up Your Sentence Power

So far, you've learned about using special words—sense words, action words, feeling words. All these add power to your writing. There are other power tools you can use, too. One of these tools is **sentence combining**.

There are many different ways to combine sentences. One easy way to start is with two words: **and** or **but**. Either of these words can change two short, choppy sentences into one longer and stronger one.

Now look at—and listen to—the differences between these "before" and "after" sentences:

1. BEFORE: She went shopping for clothes.
   She bought two sweaters.
   AFTER: She went shopping for clothes and bought two sweaters.

2. BEFORE: The dog barked at the mailman.
   It snapped at his leg.
   AFTER: The dog barked at the mailman and snapped at his leg.

3. BEFORE: My brother loves basketball.
   He plays every day.
   AFTER: My brother loves basketball and plays every day.

You can see—and hear—that the "before" sentences force you to stop and start a lot. They sound a little babyish too, don't they? When the ideas are combined in the "after" sentences, though, they sound smoother and more adult. It only takes two steps:

1. DROP THE PERIOD AT THE END OF THE FIRST SENTENCE.
2. REPLACE THE FIRST WORD OF THE SECOND SENTENCE WITH "AND".

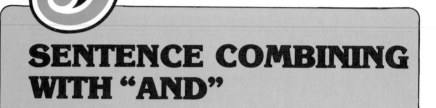

8-1 SKILL BUILDER

SENTENCE COMBINING WITH "AND"

Use these two steps to combine each of the following sentence pairs into one longer, stronger sentence.

1. Most people love a parade.
   They come early to get a good spot for watching.
2. When they get there, some of them set up folding chairs.
   They make themselves comfortable.
3. Families often bring their own food.
   They eat while they watch.
4. When the bands march by, people cheer.
   They salute the flags.
5. The music is loud.
   It's exciting to listen to.
6. The people love the sound.
   They tap their feet to the rhythm.
7. The drum majorette struts in front of the band.
   She twirls her baton.
8. The uniforms are beautiful.
   They sparkle in the sunlight.
9. Many people buy small flags.
   They wave them at the marchers.
10. After the parade, everyone feels great.
    Everyone goes home happy.

Now look at—and listen to—the differences between these "before" and "after" sentences:

1. BEFORE: She waited all day for her brother to call.
    He never did.
  AFTER: She waited all day for her brother to call, but he never did.

2. BEFORE: Letters are fun to receive.
    Surprise packages are even more fun.
  AFTER: Letters are fun to receive, but surprise packages are even more fun.

3. BEFORE: Nilda likes Johnny.
    Johnny can't stand her.
  AFTER: Nilda likes Johnny, but Johnny can't stand her.

Did you notice that in each pair of sentences there is a switch, or turn-around, in ideas? That's why you have to use **but** to combine sentences like these, and not **and**. You can do it in three steps:

---

1. CHANGE THE PERIOD AT THE END OF THE FIRST SENTENCE TO A COMMA.
2. ADD THE WORD "BUT."
3. CHANGE THE CAPITAL LETTER THAT BEGINS THE SECOND SENTENCE TO A SMALL LETTER (UNLESS THE BEGINNING WORD IS SOMEBODY'S NAME).

8-2 SKILL BUILDER: SENTENCE COMBINING WITH "BUT"

Use these three steps to combine each of the following sentence pairs into one longer, stronger sentence.

1. Bill always loved to swim.
    He wasn't very good at it.
2. He practiced all summer long.
    He didn't make the team.

3. The coach told him to keep practicing.
   Bill was too down to try.
4. He thought he would go out for football.
   He wasn't big enough.
5. His friend, Sam, said to try out for the basketball team.
   Bill wasn't tall enough.
6. Bill gave up on teams.
   He went back to swimming just for fun.
7. He swam every day.
   He didn't worry about improving.
8. He began to swim better and faster every day.
   He didn't even notice it.
9. One day, the coach told him he was ready for the team now.
   Bill could hardly believe it.
10. He thought he would fail again in the try-outs.
   This time he made it.

Trying It on Your Own

Decide whether each of the following sentence pairs should be combined with "and" or with "but." Then, combine each pair into one longer, stronger sentence according to the method you've chosen.

1. He's a big fan of his hometown baseball team.
   He never misses a game.

2. My sister asked me to mail a letter.
   We didn't have any stamps.

3. The record was a smash hit.
   It sold a million copies.

4. I love to drive.
   I hope to have my own car one day soon.

5. The day started out dark and cloudy.
   The sun broke through in the afternoon.

9 Putting It All Together

In the last few chapters, you have learned several important ways of opening up the details in your writing:

1. explaining the **what, how,** or **why** of the things you say
2. describing with **sensory words** the way things look, sound, taste, smell, or feel
3. grouping **action words** to tell more about a situation

Now here's your chance to put it all together. Take a good long look at the picture of the rock star on the next page. Think about what it might be like to be that kind of star . . . to live that kind of life . . . to go out and sing in front of all those people . . . to keep working and practicing to stay on top . . . .

How do you feel about it? How do your classmates feel? Talk it over before you write the paragraph described below the picture.

Write a paragraph that begins with one of the following sentences:

I would like to be a rock star.
I would not like to be a rock star.

Go on to explain **why** you would, or would not, enjoy a rock star's life. Tell **how** you would feel out on the stage in front of thousands of people. Tell **what** you would see and hear from that stage at a rock concert. Tell **how** you would feel about the screaming fans following you around, grabbing at your clothes, always asking for your autograph.

Don't leave any space between the opening sentence you choose to copy and your own next sentence. Try to use as many action words and sensory words as you can.

10
Getting the Right Idea

As you've probably figured out by now, every time you put together the kinds of details we've been talking about, what you get is a **paragraph**. You saw how it was done with all the details we opened up on page 29 about those strange-looking watches in Chapter Five.

You've done it yourself at least three times now. When you filled in the words about the log cabin on page 27, you completed a paragraph. When you opened up the details about the circus picture on page 38, you built up a good long paragraph of your own. When you told why you would, or wouldn't, like to be a rock star, you wrote a complete paragraph.

In these paragraphs, as in every other paragraph you will ever write, there are two big paragraph points to remember:

1. Every paragraph must be about **one main idea,** and every detail in the paragraph must be connected to that one main idea.
2. Every paragraph must begin with a **topic sentence** that lets your reader know what the main idea is.

STICKING TO YOUR MAIN IDEA

Sticking to a main idea doesn't mean saying the same thing over and over again. It does mean that you include only the details that tell more about your one main idea. Then, you open up those details as much as you can.

51

For instance, a paragraph like this one really doesn't tell much. It just repeats the main idea—a wonderful weekend— over and over again in different words.

I had a wonderful weekend. Everything about it was great. From Friday night to Sunday night, it was really super. I loved every minute of it. Boy, what a terrific time I had. It was marvelous.

What the writer of this paragraph gives us is simple repetition. What we're looking for is unity. **Unity** means adding details that tell more about one main idea.

10-1 SKILL BUILDER: CONNECTING THE RIGHT DETAILS TO THE MAIN IDEA

You can practice connecting details to a main idea with the sentences on page 53. The ideas are listed on the left side of the page. On the right is a list of details. These details are not grouped together in correct order. Each of them tells more about one of the main ideas.

Copy the first main idea in your notebook. Under it, write down all the details you can find that tell more about that one main idea.

Next, copy the second main idea. Under it, list all the details that tell more about that second main idea.

Do the same for the last main idea. Match the details carefully because each detail can be used only once.

A. Television of the future will be very different from television today.

B. Watching television can hurt your eyes unless you follow certain rules.

C. Commercials on TV can be fun to watch.

1. People will be able to "talk back" to their TV sets by pressing certain buttons.
2. Some announcers talk a mile a minute when they try to sell a product.
3. Always watch TV from a distance that is at least five times the size of the screen.
4. There will be cassettes of TV programs just as there are now cassettes of music.
5. There should be soft lighting in the room, but it shouldn't shine on the screen.
6. Sometimes advertisers use funny cartoon characters instead of real people to get viewers to buy things.
7. Turn your eyes away from the screen for a few seconds every once in a while.
8. In many TV ads, the women are beautiful, the men are handsome, and the kids are cute.
9. Many of them have catchy tunes and good singers and dancers.
10. TV sets will be so tiny that they will fit into your pocket.
11. Your TV set will be like a computer that will show all kinds of information on the screen.
12. The most important rule of all is to keep your set adjusted so that you always get a clear, steady picture.

What you just did—connecting the right details and adding them together to develop a main idea—is a very important writing skill. The more details you can connect to the main idea the better your writing will be.

Sometimes, however, it's just as important to know what to leave out as what to keep in. For example, when you filled in the words in the paragraph about the log cabin on page 27, you wrote about what you might see, smell, hear, or touch in that log cabin.

You *didn't* write that Abraham Lincoln was born in a log cabin. You might have remembered that fact, but it didn't belong in the paragraph. Including that detail would have spoiled your paragraph's unity.

In the same way, it was okay in the circus paragraph on page 38 to write about the lion tamer, the clowns, the costumes, and the food. Those are all things you see when you go to the circus.

It would not have been okay to write about the way the circus travels from town to town. Traveling is not connected to the main idea of a visit to the circus.

10-2 SKILL BUILDER: RECOGNIZING DETAILS THAT DON'T FIT THE MAIN IDEA

In this next group of sentences, you can develop your skill in choosing which details don't belong.

Read each group carefully. Decide what the main idea is. Then tell which two details don't fit because they're not directly connected to that main idea.

A. 1. Bobsled racing is one of the most exciting winter sports.
2. A four-man team steers the sled down the icy course at speeds as high as 60 miles an hour.
3. The fresh, cold air is good for you.
4. The whole team has to lean right or left with perfect timing to keep the sled from turning over on the sharp curves.
5. Many people enjoy watching dangerous sports.
6. The driver may seem to have the most important job, but it is teamwork that wins the race.

B. 1. Spring is my favorite season.
2. Yellow daffodils poke their heads up from the earth.
3. Tulips burst into a rainbow of colors.
4. Some people prefer the cold, crisp air and the clean, white snow of winter.
5. Even the rain showers are welcome because they help flowers and plants to grow.
6. One way to protect flowers from freezing is to cover them with plastic.

C. 1. We all know that smoking is bad for our health.
2. TV ads are always warning us not to smoke.
3. Many new brands of cigarettes come on the market each year.
4. It has been shown that smoking cigarettes can cause serious heart and lung diseases.
5. Hot ashes often burn holes in clothes and furniture.
6. The best thing is never to start, but if you do smoke, the next best thing is to stop right now!

D. 1. At one time, left-handed people were considered dangerous or even evil.
2. Since most people were right-handed, they thought that anyone who was so different had to be bad.
3. Today, there are special stores that sell all kinds of products made especially for "lefties."
4. Left-handed people used to be shamed and insulted by others.
5. Even parents and teachers punished young "lefties" severely if they didn't keep trying to use their right hands instead.
6. Some of the best athletes in the world are left-handed.

STARTING WITH TOPIC SENTENCES

The topic sentence is the first sentence in your paragraph. It tells your reader exactly what the whole paragraph is going to be about. The **topic sentence** states the main idea of the paragraph.

It's the topic sentence that tells us what details we can bring in. It is also the sentence that tells us what details we have to leave out. It sets the limits of all the details that go into the paragraph.

This diagram gives you an idea of how the topic sentence works.

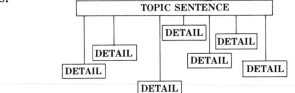

Think about this:

If a bicycle were a topic sentence, then its details could be wheels, brakes, pedals, handlebars, signal lights, a horn, or a seat. But things like rivers, boats, tunnels, and bridges surely couldn't be connected with that bicycle.

If a tree were a topic sentence, then its details could be: leaves, branches, fruit, bark, roots, and even birds and squirrels. Things like football games, a glass of milk, a taxicab, or a typewriter surely couldn't be connected with that tree.

As you can see, the topic sentence really does set the limits for the details that go into your paragraph. Thats why you want to have the very best topic sentence you can.

10-3 SKILL BUILDER: WRITING THE RIGHT DETAILS

Now you try it. Write on a separate piece of paper.

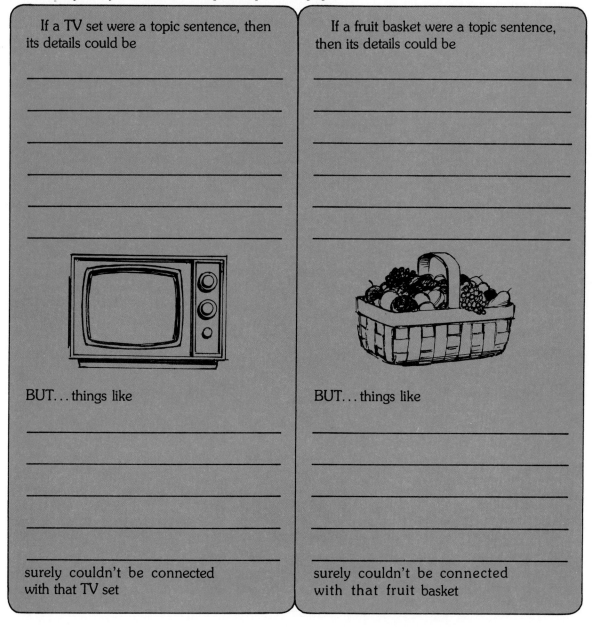

If a TV set were a topic sentence, then its details could be

_____

_____

_____

_____

_____

_____

BUT... things like

_____

_____

_____

_____

surely couldn't be connected with that TV set

If a fruit basket were a topic sentence, then its details could be

_____

_____

_____

_____

_____

_____

BUT... things like

_____

_____

_____

_____

surely couldn't be connected with that fruit basket

10-4 SKILL BUILDER: CHOOSING THE RIGHT TOPIC SENTENCE

For each of the following paragraphs, select the best topic sentence from the choices given below the paragraph.

A. _____ Even though Stevie Wonder is blind, he has become world-famous. His blindness didn't stop him from learning how to play the piano, the drums, the harmonica, and the clarinet. Stevie had his first concert when he was only twelve years old. That same year he cut a record, "Twelve-Year Old Genius," that sold a million copies. Since then, he's had many other gold records. He has appeared often on TV and has performed in front of live audiences around the world.

Topic Sentence Choices:

1. Many famous musicians have suffered from blindness.
2. Stevie Wonder plays lots of instruments.
3. Stevie Wonder has won success in spite of his handicap.

B. _____ Older brothers and sisters usually tease the youngest one. What's worse, the little one wants to be grown up, but is always treated like a baby. This often happens with parents who don't want to let go of their youngest child. In addition, the "baby" often feels left out of things that the rest of the family may be doing.

Topic Sentence Choices:

1. The youngest child usually grows up fast.
2. Being the youngest child in a family is tough.
3. Parents often spoil the youngest child.

C. _____ Each soccer team has eleven players. The teams play the game with a ball that is slightly smaller than a basketball. To score, a player must send the soccer ball flying over the goal posts. He uses only his feet and shoulders, or his head, to keep the ball moving. If any player touches the ball with his hands, the other team gets a free kick. The game is played fast and hard.

Topic Sentence Choices:

1. The game of soccer is not hard to understand.
2. Soccer is the fastest-growing sport in America today.
3. Soccer stars earn a lot of money.

WRITING THE
BEST TOPIC SENTENCE
YOU CAN

How did you decide which of the topic sentences above was the best one? Did everyone in your class agree? Let's check out one of the paragraphs to see what makes one topic sentence better than another.

Re-read the paragraph about Stevie Wonder. Here again are the three topic sentences you had to choose from:

1. Many famous musicians have suffered from blindness.

2. Stevie Wonder plays lots of instruments.

3. Stevie Wonder has won success in spite of his handicap.

Topic sentence number 1 is too big and broad for the paragraph. The details in our paragraph are not about many blind musicians. They are all about one blind musician, Stevie Wonder.

Topic sentence number 2 is too narrow for the paragraph. There is only one detail in the entire paragraph that tells us what instruments Stevie Wonder plays. What about all the other details the paragraph gives us? Topic sentence number 2 doesn't cover any of those.

Number 3, then, is clearly the best topic sentence of all. It covers all the details we are given about Stevie Wonder's blindness and about his great success. There is no detail in the paragraph that isn't connected to this topic sentence.

All this tells us something very important about the topic sentences we write on our own. **A topic sentence** must send out a **clear signal** to your reader about what details your paragraph will include.

10-5 SKILL BUILDER: WRITING A TOPIC SENTENCE THAT SIGNALS PARAGRAPH LIMITS

A. For each title given below, write a topic sentence of your own on a separate sheet of paper. Different students will, of course, come up with different sentences. Talk them over in class and decide which ones would send out the clearest signal to a reader.

    A. Travel
    B. Sports
    C. Clothes
    D. Animals

B. Read each paragraph. Then write a topic sentence in your notebook that clearly signals the details that are included in that paragraph.

1. _____ .
The problem is that young people often need more money than their parents can give them. Therefore, they take part-time jobs that will pay for new clothes or for weekend fun. Some teenagers work in supermarkets or other kinds of stores. Some pump gas at the local gas station. Others babysit. Many of them race out of school after their last class so they can get to that important job on time.

2. _____ .
City kids especially love the game. You can see them in the playgrounds at any hour of the day. They practice for hours, shooting one basket after another. They try to sink the ball from all over the court. They dribble the ball. They pass it to one another. They are very serious about improving their game.

3. _____ .
I love to look at all the beautiful Christmas decorations in the store windows. The stores are mobbed with shoppers, but people are still cheerful and smiling. I like to sing Christmas carols. My family always has a Christmas Day party. I especially love opening the beautifully wrapped presents on Christmas.

Trying It on Your Own

1. Write two sentences about the following picture that you might want to include in a paragraph about winter.

2. Now look at this topic sentence:

   > Many people gain weight in the winter.

   a. Could your two sentences fit into a paragraph that started with this topic sentence?

   b. If your answer is "yes," tell why your details would fit.

   c. If your answer is "no," write a topic sentence of your own that does cover your two details about winter.

3. Look again at the topic sentence above.

   a. Write two sentences that are connected to the main idea stated in this topic sentence.

   b. From the following list, choose five more sentences that would fit into a paragraph that started with this topic sentence.

   > In bad weather, people are often cooped up in the house.
   > They enjoy reading a good book.
   > There is nothing to do but sit around, watch TV, and eat.
   > When they do go outside, some people find that the sharp, cold air gives them a big appetite.
   > They are especially hungry for fattening, high-calorie foods that will give them quick energy.
   > Ice skating and skiing are also fun things to do in the winter.
   > All this extra food puts on pounds.

Setting Up a Scribble Sheet

What do you see in this picture? Look very carefully before you answer.

Did you start to say that all you can see is a bunch of squiggly shapes? Then did you look again and see that all the different parts are fitted together to make one complete design? Good for you! You're on your way to understanding how separate details can—and should—be grouped together.

If the artist had added just one part that was the wrong size or shape, the whole picture might have been spoiled. In the same way, just one sentence that isn't right can spoil a whole paragraph.

How do we start? How do we decide what we're going to write about? How do we think up a topic sentence that won't be too big, or too narrow, but just right? How do we tie our details right into that topic sentence?

PREPARING A SIMPLE OUTLINE

A **scribble sheet** makes a great beginning. Once you know what your paragraph has to be about, just jot down everything that comes to your mind. Don't worry yet whether your ideas fit together or not. What you scribble down doesn't have to be in any special order.

If one idea leads to another, write them both down even if you don't see a clear connection. Just let your ideas flow. Put your pen to paper and write whatever pops into your mind. The scribble sheet is the place to get down lots of details, even details you may not use later in your final paragraph. The more you write, the easier it will be to think of other ideas to add. The point is that you'll find it much easier to write that paragraph later on because you'll be able to pick and choose from many details.

---

1. JOT DOWN EVERY SINGLE THING YOU CAN THINK OF.

The scribble sheet works a little like a shopping list. Shoppers write down what they need in no particular order. Then they usually have to go hopping all over the supermarket.

You can see it would be a whole lot better to **group** similar items together. That way, no one would have to scurry from the frozen foods section of the market to the meat department and back again.

---

2. GROUP TOGETHER IDEAS THAT ARE RELATED TO EACH OTHER.

Let's see how the whole thing might work. Here's a scribble sheet you might write for a paragraph about Thanksgiving:

Thanksgiving

turkey   glazed ham.   Whole
stuffing   apple cider   family eats
gravy   Together
    cranberry sauce

                    sweet potato pie
Pilgrims   pumpkin pie
Native Americans   apple pie
They gave thanks
    for living through a tough year.

            Hassle of shopping before
Thanksgiving Day   Walnuts
Parade on TV   Oranges
                              Apples

    Kids get stuck
with washing the dishes.

Here's how these scribble sheet ideas could be grouped:

It's easy to see that the main idea here is food! You could really open up the details in a paragraph about all the delicious things that Americans eat on Thanksgiving.

The history of the holiday (Pilgrims, Native Americans) and the parade on TV have nothing to do with food, so out they go. The work of shopping before or of cleaning up afterward doesn't belong in this paragraph either. Food—glorious food—is the main idea! Writing about anything else would spoil the paragraph's unity.

Of course, it isn't always this easy. Sometimes you have to do a bit of thinking to figure out the one main idea that ties your scribble sheet details together.

11-1 SKILL BUILDER: FIGURING OUT THE MAIN IDEA

To give you some practice, here are some groups of details. Read each list carefully, one at a time. Then, write the one main idea that covers all the details in that group. The first one is done for you to show you how.

A. doesn't tell my secrets
   always ready to stand up for me
   sympathetic attitude
   understanding
   not picky or mean
   shares my interests and likes same things I do
   MAIN IDEA: What I look for in a friend

B. get lots of rest
   keep warm
   take aspirin for fever or headache
   drink plenty of liquids
   take lots of Vitamin C
   MAIN IDEA:

C. dress neatly
   no heavy make-up or unshaven face
   no fancy jewelry
   no gum-chewing
   have own pen to fill out application
   have social security number and other
      necessary information ready
   respectful attitude
   MAIN IDEA:

D. telling the truth even though it means you'll be punished
   standing up to someone who is bigger and stronger than you are
   deciding to stop smoking even though you know how hard it will be
   refusing to go along with the crowd even though it means being called "chicken"
   MAIN IDEA:

E. check ads for sales
   buy only at stores that give refunds or make exchanges
   don't be fooled by fancy advertising
   buy supermarket items when they are on "special"
   shop different stores to find the best prices
   MAIN IDEA: _____

F. loneliness
   sickness
   lack of money
   old friends dying off
   children and grandchildren moving away
   no respect from younger people
   fear of being robbed or mugged
   MAIN IDEA: _____

Trying It on Your Own

Here are some topics about which you probably have lots to say:

A. Movies

B. New Year's Eve

C. Teachers

D. Being Popular

E. Teenage Fads

For each of these topics, do these four things:

1. Make up a scribble sheet.

2. Group together related details.

3. Write the main idea that ties together the biggest group of details.

4. Cross out the details that do not fit the main idea.

Finding the Clue in the Paragraph Title

As you've seen, the scribble sheet can show you what you should write about in your paragraph. Lots of times the paragraph title itself gives you a headstart.

Titles can often point your thinking in the right direction. You might not be entirely sure what this picture is all about, for instance, until you saw its title, "Industry." Then, all the details would click into place, and you'd recognize that it's a painting of a factory.

The title of a paragraph can do the same thing for you. It can tell you not only what to write about, but how to write it. There are title clues that you can find for all three types of writing that you do.

1. telling about something that happened
2. describing something or someone
3. explaining what you think or how you feel about something

A title like "My Worst Moment" would clue you in to tell about what happened.

A title like "My School Cafeteria" would clue you in to describe the sights, sounds, and smells of your cafeteria.

12·1

SKILL BUILDER

KNOWING WHEN TO TELL AND WHEN TO DESCRIBE

Here are five other paragraph titles to check out. Would you write a story or write a description for each one?

1. My Room Is A Mess
2. The Time I Forgot My Keys
3. My First Date
4. The Street Where I Live
5. The Worst Nightmare I Ever Had

What would you do, however, with a title like "Ways to Improve Your Looks"?

There's no story to tell. There is nothing to describe. You have to *explain* what things people can do to become better-looking.

KNOWING HOW TO EXPLAIN

In titles like the one above, there's often a special **clue word** that tells you what to do. Let's use some other titles to see how these clue words work.

1. Title: "Why I Love Saturday Night"
   Clue Word: Why
   What To Do: Give Reasons

2. Title: "Causes of Accidents"
   Clue Word: Causes (Another Word for Reasons)
   What To Do: Explain What Creates or Brings About the Situation

3. Title: "Results of Dropping Out of School"
   Clue Word: Results
   What To Do: Explain What Happens Because of the Situation

4. Title: "Effects of Smoking"
   Clue Word: Effects (Another Word for Results)
   What To Do: Explain What Happens Because of the Situation

5. Title: "How to Get Around My Mother"
   Clue Word: How
   What To Do: Tell What to Do (Methods or Ways)

6. Title: "Ways to Train a Pet"
   Clue Word: Ways
   What To Do: Tell How to Do It (Ways)

7. Title: "Problems with My Budget"
   Clue Word: Problems
   What To Do: Explain What the Problems Are and Why They Are a Hassle

You can see how helpful it is when the clue words are right in the title this way. Memorize the clue words. They will help you take another big step toward knowing what to write.

CLUE WORD	WHAT TO DO
why	give reasons
causes	explain what creates or brings about the situation
results	explain what happens because of the situation
effects	explain what happens because of the situation
how	tell what to do (methods or ways)
ways	tell how to do it (ways)
problems	explain what the problems are and why they're a hassle

RECOGNIZING HIDDEN TITLE CLUES

Sometimes the clue word is hidden in the title. Then you have to be a good detective and spot it anyway.

Think about a title like "When Mothers Work."

What happens when mothers work? There are certain effects on the family when mothers work, aren't there? What's the hidden clue word? **Effects.** What should you do? Explain what happens when mothers work outside the home.

Another title might be "High School Is Not What I Expected."

Why isn't it what you expected? What's the hidden clue word this time? **Why?** What should you do? Give reasons why high school isn't what you expected.

How about "Should Boys Help with Housework?"

This title asks for your opinion. When you give an opinion, you have to tell why you think as you do. You have to give the reasons for your opinion. What's the hidden clue word, then? **Why?** What should you do? Tell your opinion and give reasons.

There is one other kind of title that gives you two things to talk about at the same time. Here are some examples of these kinds of titles:

Going to School Is the Same As Working At a Job
Soccer Is Very Much Like Football
TV Cops and Real-Life Cops
City Life Is More Exciting Than Country Life
Family Life Is Not What It Used to Be

The hidden clue in titles like these is the fact that there are two things to write about. Your job is to explain how the two things are the same, or explain how the two things are different.

When you tell how two things are similar, you are writing a **comparison**. When you tell how they are different, you're writing a **contrast**.

Trying It on Your Own

For each of the titles on this chart, fill in the clue words and tell what to do. Refer to the chart on page 71 if you need help. Don't forget that some of the clue words may be hidden.

TITLE	CLUE WORD	WHAT TO DO
How to Give a Surprise Party		
Problems With My Family		
Results of Being Overweight		
Effects of Being Out Of Work		
Should Women Be Firefighters?		
Causes of Crime		
Ways to Earn Money		
Should Students Grade Teachers?		

13

Building Up Your Sentence Power

Remember that important power tool for writing called **sentence combining?** In Chapter Eight, you learned how to use **and** and **but** to help you build one long, strong sentence out of two choppy little ones. Another pair of words that can help you do the same thing is **who** and **which.**

When you want to build a longer, stronger sentence about a person, you can use the word **who.** When you want to build a longer, stronger sentence about a thing, you can use the word **which.** Here's how these words work. Now look at—and listen to—the differences between these "before" and "after" sentences.

1. BEFORE: Mr. Cabot teaches history.
   He is getting married soon.
   AFTER: Mr. Cabot, who teaches history, is getting married soon.

2. BEFORE: My friend is only sixteen.
   He will be graduating in June.
   AFTER: My friend, who is only sixteen, will be graduating in June.

3. BEFORE: Roger played football in college.
   He would love to turn pro.
   AFTER: Roger, who played football in college, would love to turn pro.

Did you spot the pattern? In the "after" sentence of each pair, one word (*who*) was added, and one word was dropped. Here's how:

---

1. ADD A COMMA AND THE WORD "WHO" RIGHT AFTER THE SUBJECT IN THE FIRST SENTENCE. (THE SUBJECT IS THE PART THAT TELLS YOU WHO OR WHAT THE SENTENCE IS ABOUT.)
2. CHANGE THE PERIOD AT THE END OF THE FIRST SENTENCE TO A COMMA.
3. DROP THE FIRST WORD OF THE SECOND SENTENCE. THEN, ADD ON THE REST OF THE SECOND SENTENCE TO SENTENCE NUMBER ONE.

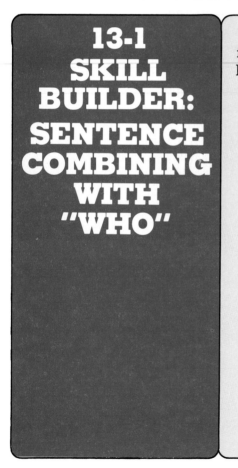

13-1 SKILL BUILDER: SENTENCE COMBINING WITH "WHO"

Use these three steps to combine each of the following sentence pairs into one longer, stronger sentence.

1. Mrs. Wells is very understanding.
   She is my favorite teacher.
2. My father was very sick last year.
   He has to be extra careful about his health.
3. My neighbors have sold their house.
   They will move south next week.
4. Mike dances beautifully.
   He goes to a disco three or four nights a week.
5. Diane loves to fix machines.
   She is the only girl in the machine shop class.
6. Charles is the tallest boy in the class.
   He is on the basketball team.
7. The witnesses had seen the accident.
   They were called to testify.
8. My friend is very good in math.
   She works as a bank teller.
9. The store clerk is very friendly.
   He always greets customers with a smile.

Now look at—and listen to—the differences between these "before" and "after" sentences:

1. BEFORE: Our TV set has been fixed twice already.
            It is broken again.
   AFTER: Our TV set, which has been fixed twice already, is broken again.

2. BEFORE: The car had been repainted.
            It looked almost like new again.
   AFTER: The car, which had been repainted, looked almost like new again.

3. BEFORE: That movie has many stars and great music.
            It is a big hit.
   AFTER: That movie, which has many stars and great music, is a big hit.

You can see that the pattern is the same as before. In the "after" sentence of each pair, one word (*which*) was added, and one word was dropped.

Here are the three steps:

1. ADD A COMMA AND THE WORD "WHICH" RIGHT AFTER THE SUBJECT IN THE FIRST SENTENCE.
2. CHANGE THE PERIOD AT THE END OF THE FIRST SENTENCE TO A COMMA.
3. DROP THE FIRST WORD OF THE SECOND SENTENCE. THEN, ADD ON THE REST OF THE SECOND SENTENCE TO SENTENCE NUMBER ONE.

13-2
SKILL BUILDER:

SENTENCE COMBINING WITH "WHICH"

Use these three steps to combine each of these sentence pairs into one longer, stronger sentence.

1. Our kitten was born only a few weeks ago.
   It is still shy around people.
2. Food costs are very high now.
   They are going up more every day.
3. The park is dark and deserted.
   It is no place to go walking alone.
4. Air pollution is a serious problem.
   It is caused by the fumes from cars and trucks.
5. The apartment was small and noisy.
   It was crowded with people.
6. Those boots are made of real leather.
   They cost over a hundred dollars.
7. The sky was dark with clouds.
   It warned us that a storm was on the way.
8. The fire burned for more than two hours.
   It completely destroyed the building.
9. Old movies can be fun to watch.
   They are shown on TV every once in a while.
10. Jogging is a big sport today.
    It can be done by people of all ages.

Trying It on Your Own

Decide whether each of the following sentence pairs should be combined with "who" or "which". Then, combine each pair into a longer, stronger sentence according to the method you've learned.

1. Magic delights many people.
   It takes years of practice to learn.

2. Houdini was a world-famous magician.
   He could even make an elephant disappear.

3. Houdini trained himself to control his breathing.
   He could stay underwater for a long time.

4. Chains were tied around locked metal trunks.
   They never stopped him from doing his underwater escape act.

5. Magicians are always trying to improve their act.
   They still copy some of Houdini's great tricks.

14 Putting It All Together

In the last several chapters, you have learned a great deal about paragraph organization. You know now that you must have:

1. one **main idea** to which all your details are related
2. a **topic sentence** that clearly signals your main idea

You also know how to use:

a **scribble sheet**
the **clue** in the paragraph title

This picture will give you a chance to put it all together. Study it carefully. What does it make you think of? A storm? A

starlit night? The beauty of nature? Outer space? Unidentified Flying Objects?

You could write a paragraph about this picture with any one of these titles:

A. The Most Beautiful Night of My Life
B. Why People Are Fascinated by U.F.O.'s
C. When A Big Storm Strikes
D. Ways to Enjoy the Beauties of Nature
E. Problems of Exploring Outer Space

Choose the title you like best and make up a scribble sheet for it. Jot down all the details you can think of. Then, check the title clue to see what kind of details you should be concentrating on. Be sure you have them on your scribble sheet. Next, group your details and find your main idea. Finally, write a good, strong topic sentence that clearly signals your main idea.

15
Writing the Paragraph: Telling a Story

Story-telling is the kind of writing you probably know best. You've been listening to stories, and telling stories, since you were a small child. Story-telling comes naturally to all of us.

You're telling a story when you talk about something that happened to you at home or outside. You're telling a story when

you tell about something you did. You're telling a story when you talk about things that have happened to your family or your friends.

A picture like the one on **page 80** might remind you of something that once happened to you when a teacher sent you to the board. You could write a story about it.

Here's a story that one student did write about a funny classroom experience that happened to him.

The wildest thing happened to me in history class last week. First of all, I was tired. I didn't get much sleep the night before. My next-door neighbors were hollering and screaming at each other until three o'clock in the morning. Second, I didn't have my homework. I couldn't get anything done at home with all that noise next door. Sure enough, Mrs. Wilson sent me to the board to write the date the Saxon Wars began. Of course, I didn't know. I figured all I could do was make a joke of it. I just scribbled down yesterday's date, when the war next door had started. I scrawled 916, meaning September 16th. Imagine my shock when Mrs. Wilson gave me a big smile and a big check on the board. The Saxon Wars really did begin in the year 916! That sure was the luckiest guess I ever made in my life!

BUILDING UP YOUR WORD POWER: TIME WORDS

In the story above, the writer tells us he was tired and unprepared because of what had happened at home the night before. Then, he tells us the teacher sent him to the board. Finally, he tells us how he got out of the situation—much to his own surprise.

If he had told us these things in a different order, his story wouldn't have made any sense. Starting at the beginning and telling what happened step by step means using **time order**.

Usually, we can all use time order without any trouble. We use words like first, second, and third all the time. This is one way to show the time order in which things happen. Using the same words over and over again, however, makes writing very boring. That's why there are plenty of other **time words,** like the ones in the box, for us to use that also show time order:

after	following this	next
afterward	immediately	once
at last	in the meantime	since then
before	later	then
finally	meanwhile	while

15-1 SKILL BUILDER: RECOGNIZING TIME WORDS WHEN YOU SEE THEM

Read the following story. Identify all the time words.

The bank in my neighborhood once got held up. Before the robber could get away, the bank guard rang the secret alarm. The thief immediately grabbed four people as hostages. He showed them he had a gun. In the meantime, the police arrived. They tried to get the gunman to give up, but he wouldn't do it. Then, the gunman told the police he wanted the money he had stolen and a fast getaway car in front of the bank within one hour. Meanwhile, he would not release the hostages. The next thing the police tried was tear gas. That didn't work either. Finally, they called in a priest. While the priest was talking to the robber, one policeman climbed up to the low roof of the bank. Following this, the getaway car was driven up outside the bank. After the robber saw the car, he thought he had won. He came out the door, pushing the four hostages in front of him. Immediately, the police officer on the roof leaped onto the robber's back, knocking him to the sidewalk. Police closed in from everywhere. Afterward, the cuffs were snapped on the gunman's wrists, and he was taken away. The excitement was over, and all the hostages were safe. Later that night I saw the whole thing again on the TV news. Since then, I'm pretty careful when I go into a bank. I take a good look around to see who else is in there.

Did you catch all 15 time words used in the story? Which one was used twice? Did you also spot the commas that came after the time words when they started sentences by themselves?

In the meantime, the police arrived.
Finally, they called in a priest.
Afterward, the cuffs were snapped on the gunman's wrists. . . .

BUT

Later that night I saw the whole thing again on the TV news.

This comma rule is an important one to remember:

PUT A COMMA AFTER A TIME WORD WHEN IT STANDS BY ITSELF AT THE BEGINNING OF YOUR SENTENCE.

15-2 SKILL BUILDER: ARRANGING STORIES IN CORRECT TIME ORDER

Below are groups of sentences that will tell a story when you put them in the right time order. Re-arrange each group of sentences into a paragraph that makes sense. Use the time words in each sentence to figure out what the correct time order of the story should be.

A. 1. Shaking with fear, Maria slipped out of her bed.
   2. The "burglar" was her cat, walking through the broken pieces of the glass lamp it had knocked over in the dark.
   3. Before she could move, there was another sound, like footsteps, in the room.
   4. At last, her fright was over.
   5. There was a sudden loud crash.
   6. Then, she felt her way along the wall to the light switch.
   7. Immediately, Maria woke up from a sound sleep.
   8. Finally, she found the switch and turned on the lights.

B. 1. While I was cleaning up the food, Teddy pulled out every toy he had.
   2. Meanwhile, I was going crazy trying to shut him up and clean up all at the same time.
   3. The worst job I ever had was babysitting for my little cousin, Teddy.
   4. Following this, he threw the broken toy pieces all over the place.
   5. The first thing he did was dump all the cans and boxes of food out of the cabinets onto the floor.
   6. Since then, I have refused to babysit for Teddy.
   7. Afterward, he began bawling and sobbing because he didn't have any more toys.
   8. Next, he started to take the toys apart.

C. 1. At last, Kev was well enough to travel, and they left.
   2. After we met, we hung out together all the time.
   3. Once I had a real buddy named Kevin.
   4. In the meantime, his parents got ready to move out West.
   5. While he was in the hospital, I went to see him every day.
   6. I never saw my buddy again.
   7. Then, Kev suddenly got real sick.
   8. The doctors said the air out there would be better for Kev.
   9. Later, he came home, but he still had to stay in bed for two more months.

BUILDING UP YOUR WORD POWER: MORE ACTION WORDS

You've heard the saying, "Actions speak louder than words." You also learned in Chapter Four that action words speak louder than everyday words. In the story on page 81, for instance, the writer used action words like *hollering* and *screaming* instead of an everyday word like "arguing." He used *scribbled* and *scrawled* instead of "wrote." These action words helped to make the story vivid and real for us.

Everyday words are okay, but we can get very tired of them if we use the same ones all the time. There are four everyday words—tell, look, walk, and annoy—that are used much too often. There are other stronger and louder action words that you can use in their place, depending on the "sense" of the sentence. You may already know some of these action words. Others may be new to you.

15-3 SKILL BUILDER: CHOOSING THE BEST ACTION WORD

Complete the sentences below each group of action words by filling in the word that best fits the sentence. Write the words in your notebook.

Instead of TELL

whisper: to speak very softly so others can't hear

warn: to notify or signal something bad or dangerous

gossip: to repeat unfriendly talk or rumors

advise: to give suggestions or helpful hints to someone.

1. I always _____ my boyfriend that fast driving will cause an accident.
2. My neighbors always stand around and _____ about everyone else on the block.
3. I tried to _____ the answer to my friend, but the teacher heard me anyhow.
4. I know how to get around my parents, so I always _____ my brother about what he should say to them.

Instead of LOOK

stare: to look steadily, or for a long time

glare: to look angrily

glance: to look quickly and then turn away

inspect: to look carefully and closely

gaze: to look with love or longing

1. He only had time to _____ at the morning newspaper because he had to rush off to work.
2. My mother always _____ the washing instructions on a dress or a blouse before she buys it.
3. Everyone got a kick out of seeing the bride and groom _____ into each other's eyes before they kissed.
4. She was so surprised to see her best friend on TV that all she could do was _____ at the screen with her mouth open.
5. The captain would _____ at the new soldiers when they didn't salute him.

85

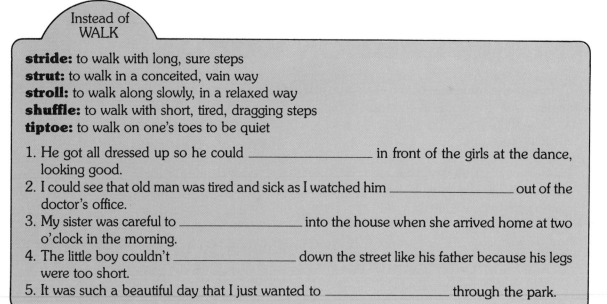

Instead of WALK

stride: to walk with long, sure steps
strut: to walk in a conceited, vain way
stroll: to walk along slowly, in a relaxed way
shuffle: to walk with short, tired, dragging steps
tiptoe: to walk on one's toes to be quiet

1. He got all dressed up so he could _____ in front of the girls at the dance, looking good.
2. I could see that old man was tired and sick as I watched him _____ out of the doctor's office.
3. My sister was careful to _____ into the house when she arrived home at two o'clock in the morning.
4. The little boy couldn't _____ down the street like his father because his legs were too short.
5. It was such a beautiful day that I just wanted to _____ through the park.

Instead of ANNOY

tease: to make fun of someone with mean remarks
nag: to annoy someone with constant complaints
pester: to bother someone over and over
irritate: to make someone impatient or angry
disturb: to interrupt or interfere with someone's peace and quiet

1. No one was allowed to _____ the baby when he was having his nap.
2. Her mother would constantly _____ her about her schoolwork and marks.
3. During the summer, mosquitoes can really _____ people who want to sit outdoors.
4. The older children sometimes _____ the younger ones and make them cry.
5. I can always _____ my father by just asking him for money.

86

Trying It on Your Own

1. Complete the following story by filling in the blanks with the missing time words. Look at page 82 if you need help.

My father _____ told me the story of how he got his job at Western Union. About 50 other men were there to apply for the same job. _____, everyone took a number. _____, they all filled out an application form. _____, a man from the company was taking notes on all the men and how they looked. _____ they filled out the applications, the men were told to wait till their numbers were called. _____ they were waiting, the telegraph machine in the office started to click. Those machines send out their messages in beeping sounds. In Morse Code, the sounds stand for the letters of words. My father _____ jumped up and ran into the manager's office. _____, he came out of the office as the new assistant manager. Why did he rush in before his turn? The message that office machine had clicked out was that anyone who wanted the job should come in right now. Of the 50 men there, my dad was the only one sharp enough to realize that the clicking sounds were in Morse Code!

2. Complete the following story by changing each word in parentheses to a better, stronger action word.

I'll never forget my first day as a counselor in a day camp. First, my group lined up so I could (look at) them carefully. I knew immediately that I had trouble. I thought I could (walk) from one kid to another, nice and easy, and get to know them. Instead, I had to (walk) quickly toward them before they could run away. I decided I'd better (tell) them how to behave, but no one listened. One kid just (looked) at me like I had two heads. Next, another one (walked) out in front of the group, pretending he was top man. In the meantime, I could hear the other kids giggling and (talking) about me to each other. Finally, I (looked) at them as hard as I could, and ordered everyone down to the pool. Of course, they (walked) along like little old men just to (annoy) me. They would (look) at me quickly and then start to giggle some more. Later, at the pool, they did everything they could think of to (annoy) me again. They (walked) behind my back to the diving board after I (told) them to keep off. They kept (annoying) one little boy who was too fat to swim fast. I kept (looking) at my watch, longing for this work day to end. When at last it did, eight hours later, I went home and collapsed.

3. Choose any three of the following titles. For each one, write a story of your own in clear time order. Use as many time words and action words as you can.

   a. The Worst Moment of My Life
   b. A Funny Thing Happened to Me on the Way to School
   c. The Day I Really Grew Up
   d. The Beginning of a Beautiful Friendship
   e. When I Got Into Trouble
   f. My Most Enjoyable Christmas
   g. The Day I Was Locked Out of My House
   h. The Time the Laugh Was on Me

16
Building Up Your Sentence Power

Still another way of combining two short sentences into a longer, stronger one is to use "-ing" on an action word.

Now look at—and listen to—the differences between these "before" and "after" sentences:

---

1. BEFORE: He jumped on his bike.
   He rode away quickly.
   AFTER: Jumping on his bike, he rode away quickly.

---

2. BEFORE: She shivered from the cold.
   She turned up the heat.
   AFTER: Shivering from the cold, she turned up the heat.

---

3. BEFORE: He walked out into the sunshine.
   He felt as free as a bird.
   AFTER: Walking out into the sunshine, he felt as free as a bird.

The pattern is easy to follow. To combine sentences this way, you have to build a word that ends in "-ing." This is how:

> 1. DROP THE FIRST WORD IN THE FIRST SENTENCE.
> 2. ADD THE LETTERS "ING" TO THE SECOND WORD AND CAPITALIZE THAT WORD.
> 3. CHANGE THE PERIOD AT THE END OF THE FIRST SENTENCE TO A COMMA.
> 4. CHANGE THE CAPITAL LETTER THAT BEGINS THE SECOND SENTENCE TO A SMALL LETTER (UNLESS THE BEGINNING WORD IS SOMEBODY'S NAME). THEN, ADD ON THE REST OF THE SECOND SENTENCE TO SENTENCE NUMBER ONE.

89

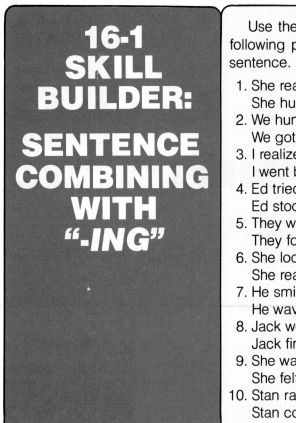

16-1 SKILL BUILDER: SENTENCE COMBINING WITH "-ING"

Use these four steps to combine each of the following pairs of sentences into one longer, stronger sentence.

1. She realized she didn't have any milk in the house.
   She hurried to the store to buy some.
2. We hunted for an old book in the library.
   We got dusty and dirty.
3. I realized I had forgotten my umbrella.
   I went back home to get one.
4. Ed tried to look calm and cool.
   Ed stood up to make his speech.
5. They watched the movie.
   They forgot all about the time.
6. She looked around the strange street.
   She realized she was lost.
7. He smiled happily.
   He waved to the crowd.
8. Jack worked hard to fix his car.
   Jack finally finished the job at midnight.
9. She watched the children laugh and play.
   She felt good.
10. Stan raced down the hall.
    Stan collided with the school principal.

Trying It on Your Own

This time, you add a second short sentence to the first one you're given. Then, combine each pair of short sentences into one longer, stronger sentence according to the "-ing" method you've learned.

SAMPLE: We enjoyed the funny story.
ADD: We laughed out loud.
COMBINE: Enjoying the funny story, we laughed out loud.

1. Dad put on his hat and coat.

2. She danced at the wedding.

3. I spotted my friend across the street.

4. He practiced the drums two hours a day.

5. Brenda dived into the pool.

17

Writing the Paragraph: Describing a Person or a Place

Read the following newspaper article. What makes this description such a good one? The writer filled it with the kinds of sensory words and action words that make writing come alive.

Playground Is Alive with Running Water and Soaked Children

NEW YORK, June 30—The new Water Playground in the southwest corner of Central Park is a place for children to play.

Little streams of water run down cement ramps and trickle around rough stone mounds. Water spurts out of the jungle gym and pours down the wet, gleaming slides. A waterfall tumbles down into a round wading pool below.

Laughing kids dance in and out of the sprinklers. They zoom down the slippery slides. They climb all over the jungle gym, ducking the water spraying from the center. Tiny tots dip fat little fingers into the wading pool. Some of them run through the water, making squishy sounds and splashing wildly as they go.

As the hour gets later, the playground gets quieter. The shadows change and deepen. The leaves on the trees darken to black-green velvet. Tired and happy, the children go home.

Ever since Chapter Two, you have been using sensory words to describe the way things look, sound, taste, smell, or feel. In Chapters Five, Six, and Seven, you learned about opening up the details to paint a vivid word picture for your reader. These are just the things this newspaper reporter did, too. You can almost see that water, hear the laughing children, and feel that cold, wet slide.

Look at the way the reporter opened up the details. She could have said only that everything in the playground is built around water. Instead, she opened up the details wide by using many action words to describe the water:

streams that run and trickle,
water that spurts and pours,
and a waterfall that tumbles into a pool below.

Through the exercises in this book, you have already written many good descriptions of your own. The more of these paragraphs you write, the stronger your powers of description will grow.

WRITING A CHARACTER SKETCH

A **character sketch** is a special kind of description. In a character sketch, you are describing a person. To get across what that person is really like, you still need to use sensory words and action words. You also need to deal with feeling. (Look again at Chapter Three.)

When you describe a person, you want to do more than just tell what that person looks like. You want to show what kind of human being that person is—kind, gentle, wise, mean, cruel, and so on. To do all this, you have to open up the details as much as you can.

Study the woman in this picture. The following description is of a woman very much like her. Notice how the writer tells us about his grandmother's size, the color of her eyes, her rough hands and soft face. Notice, too, how he tells us more than this about her. He tells us what she was like and how he felt about her. He opens up the details.

93

My grandmother was my favorite human being. The only time I ever saw her cry was when Grandpa died. Tiny and hunched over in her black widow's dress, she wept for the man she had shared her life with for almost 50 years. It was a hard life, too, but Grandma never complained. She wasn't much more than five feet tall, but she was strong and wiry. She cleaned other people's houses for many years, but still found time to cook and bake for us. Her coal-black eyes usually twinkled with laughter. When I didn't mind my manners, though, those eyes could blaze with anger. She never stayed mad for long. After a few minutes, she'd hand me a fresh-baked cookie or tell me a story about some stunt she'd pulled in her own childhood. Her voice was much louder than you'd expect from such a little woman. Many times she made me jump when she bellowed my name. She could also be gentle and tender. Her hands were rough and hard from years of work, but they were soft whenever they touched me. Her cheeks were soft, too. They were wrinkled, but they felt like silk. When she died at the age of 71, she was buried next to Grandpa. I've missed her every day since.

BUILDING UP YOUR WORD POWER: GETTING RID OF EMPTY WORDS

Suppose the writer of the paragraph above had written that his grandmother was a "nice" woman or a "great" person. Would you have the same clear picture of her in your mind that you have now? Of course you wouldn't. That's because words like nice and great don't really describe anything clearly. They're empty words that we just shove in anywhere.

We say, "It's a nice day" when we talk about the weather. We tell our friends that they look nice when they're all dressed up. We talk about a nice house, or a nice girl, or a nice piece of meat in the market!

We go to a great party, or we see a great movie. We eat a great meal, and we describe a great dancer.

Throw away those empty words! There are other words that you can use instead to paint a fuller picture.

INSTEAD OF NICE:
1. when you mean pleasing or satisfying: **pleasant; enjoyable; delightful**
2. when you mean friendly, easy to be with: **agreeable; amiable; sociable**
3. when you mean good-looking: **handsome; stunning; attractive**
4. when you mean kind, understanding: **sympathetic; compassionate; warm-hearted**

INSTEAD OF GREAT:
1. when you mean good at something: **skilled; expert; talented**
2. when you mean very good or excellent; **marvelous; splendid; magnificent**
3. when you mean exciting: **thrilling; sensational; wonderful**
4. when you mean big and impressive: **noble; stately; majestic**

17-1 SKILL BUILDER: EXCHANGING EMPTY WORDS FOR FULL ONES

In each sentence below, change <u>nice</u> or <u>great</u> to one of the better, fuller words.

1. Lily is a nice person who always has a smile for everyone.
2. The bridge looks great when it's lit up at night.
3. He's so great with his hands that he can build anything.
4. The cool air at the beach is nice after the heat of the city.
5. Mrs. Harmon is such a nice teacher that all the kids love her.
6. Alan always comes up with great ideas for partying and having fun.
7. She plays a great game of tennis.
8. When my mother wears make-up, she looks really nice.
9. The ride on the Cyclone is so great that I always go back for more.
10. It's nice on my block in the spring because we have a lot of trees.

Trying It on Your Own

Choose any three of the paragraph titles below. For each one, write a paragraph of description. Start with a scribble sheet. Use as many sensory words and action words as you can. See if you can use some of the words from the lists on pages 85 and 86, too. Try to make the person or place you're describing come alive for your reader.

1. The Rottenest Kid I Know

2. My Favorite Amusement Park

3. A Person I'll Always Remember

4. Our School Cafeteria

5. My Mother

6. A Snowstorm

7. My Most Interesting Friend

8. The Most Beautiful Place I've Seen

18
Building Up
Your Sentence Power

Think you've just about covered everything there is to know about sentence combining? Not quite! There is yet another good way to combine short sentences. You can use **describing words**.

Now look at—and listen to—the differences between these "before" and "after" sentences:

---

1. BEFORE: The floor was waxed.
The floor was polished.
The floor looked beautiful.

   AFTER: Waxed and polished, the floor looked beautiful.

---

2. BEFORE: The puppies are cute.
The puppies are frisky.
The puppies are fun to watch.

   AFTER: Cute and frisky, the puppies are fun to watch.

---

3. BEFORE: The audience was thrilled.
The audience was amazed.
The audience watched the magician's tricks.

   AFTER: Thrilled and amazed, the audience watched the magician's tricks.

You can see the pattern. Everything but the last word in the first two sentences is dropped. Then these two describing words are put together to build a longer, stronger sentence. This is how it's done:

---

1. DROP EVERYTHING BUT THE LAST DESCRIBING WORD IN THE FIRST TWO SENTENCES.
2. CONNECT THESE TWO DESCRIBING WORDS WITH "AND."
3. CAPITALIZE THE FIRST DESCRIBING WORD AND PUT A COMMA AFTER THE SECOND DESCRIBING WORD.
4. CHANGE THE CAPITAL LETTER THAT BEGINS THE THIRD SENTENCE TO A SMALL LETTER (UNLESS THE BEGINNING WORD IS SOMEBODY'S NAME). THEN, ADD THIS LAST SENTENCE TO THE TWO DESCRIBING WORDS.

18-1 SKILL BUILDER: SENTENCE COMBINING WITH DESCRIBING WORDS

Use these four steps to combine each of the following groups of sentences into one longer, stronger sentence.

1. The car was dented.
   The car was scratched.
   The car could only be sold for scrap.

2. The doctor was famous.
   The doctor was respected.
   The doctor had many patients.

3. The fans were disgusted.
   The fans were disappointed.
   The fans booed their team.

4. He was tired.
   He was hungry.
   He was glad to get home.

5. The TV program was funny.
   The TV program was lively.
   The TV program became one of the most popular of the year.

6. She was respected.
   She was trusted.
   She was promoted to the position of sales manager.

7. The photograph was clear.
   The photograph was sharp.
   The photograph won first prize in the contest.

8. We were surprised.
   We were delighted.
   We accepted the invitation to the party.

9. Bobby was confused.
   Bobby was puzzled.
   Bobby couldn't figure out how to do the math problem.

10. The movie star was thrilled.
    The movie star was excited.
    The movie star accepted the Oscar.

Trying It on Your Own

Now add a third sentence to the first two that you're given below. Then, combine each sentence group into one longer, stronger sentence according to the method you've learned in this chapter.

SAMPLE: The streets were flooded.
            The streets were cracked.

ADD: The streets need a major repair job.

COMBINE: Flooded and cracked, the streets need a major repair job.

1. The music was loud.
   The music was fast.

2. Carol was happy.
   Carol was proud.

3. The turkey was stuffed.
   The turkey was roasted.

4. The dancer was graceful.

   The dancer was talented.

5. The suitcase was closed.

   The suitcase was locked.

Writing the Paragraph: Explaining What You Think or How You Feel

When you discovered the secret of the clue words in Chapter Twelve, you also discovered that there were five basic ways to explain something:

1. TELLING THE RESULTS (when the clue word is "results" or "effects")
2. EXPLAINING METHODS OR WAYS (when the clue word is "how" or "ways")
3. TELLING WHAT THE PROBLEMS ARE AND WHY THEY ARE A HASSLE (when the clue word is "problems")
4. GIVING REASONS (when the clue word is "why" or "causes")
5. COMPARING AND CONTRASTING (when the hidden clue in the title tells you to write about two things at the same time)

The best way to get started on any of them is with a scribble sheet. Remember, the important thing at first is just to jot down ideas. Grouping comes later. Then you'll know which ideas to keep and which to throw out. Grouping will also show you which one is your main idea. After that, you can write a topic sentence that covers all the details you want to include in your paragraph.

Here is an example of a paragraph developed by telling results:

The Results of War
Clue word: results

Many innocent people suffer in wartime. Two results of war, of course, are death and destruction. Enemy bombs rain down on cities and towns. Helpless women and children run screaming into the night, but they can't escape. Their homes go up in flames around them. Also, people starve because their food supplies are cut off. Sometimes the soldiers grab all the food for themselves. Other times enemy gunfire blows up farms and food stores. The worst result of all is that families are smashed forever. Husbands, fathers, brothers, and sons die in battle. Therefore, the pain of innocent people goes on after wars end.

19-1
SKILL BUILDER: PREDICTING THE OUTCOME

When you're dealing with results or effects, you are really talking about the outcome of a situation. You have to ask yourself, "What happens when...?" or "What would happen if...?"

Here are a few practice situations. For each one, fill in a possible result in your notebook.

Situation   Possible Result or Outcome

1. If people smoke a lot, they may   _____
                                              _____

2. When you eat too much at dinner, you   _____
   may   _____

3. When parents see a bad report card, they   _____
                                              _____

4. If a movie becomes a blockbuster success, _____
                                              _____

5. If prices keep rising,   _____
                                              _____

6. If machines continue to take over more   _____
   and more jobs,   _____

7. When a family moves from the country to   _____
   a big city,   _____

8. When people lose their jobs,   _____
                                              _____

9. If a husband brings home guests for   _____
   dinner without asking his wife first,

10. If two people get married without know-   _____
    ing each other too well,

Here is an example of a paragraph developed by explaining ways:

© 1968 United Feature Syndicate, Inc.

Ways to Win a Valentine
Clue word: ways

There are many unusual ways to win a valentine. Anyone can send just a valentine card or a gift. Instead, how about renting a huge billboard and having your valentine message printed on it? You might say something like: "Gene, I love you. Be my valentine. Julie." Another way might be to hire a small airplane to write a valentine message in smoke across the sky. In big, white, floating letters, the smoke could spell out: "Dave loves Susan." With enough money, you could also buy time on a local radio station. Then you'd be able to broadcast a message to your valentine every hour on the hour all through Valentine's Day. You can see that winning a valentine can be fun as well as romantic.

103

Here is an example of a paragraph developed by telling the problem:

The Problem of Being A Woman Today
Clue word: problem

Women today are being pulled in two directions at the same time. On the one hand, they love their families. They want to be good wives and mothers. On the other hand, TV, movies, and magazines pound them with the idea that they should have a career. That's fine if they want a career. If they don't, they still get the message that there is something wrong with them. Many women even feel ashamed to say they are only housewives. Nevertheless, raising children and making a good home for them are important, too. TV and movies should show this. They should make women feel that whichever choice they make can be the right one.

TELLING WHY WITH REASONS

It's important to be able to recognize a real reason when you see one. Sometimes we write a reason which isn't really a reason at all. It might only be another way of saying the first part of the sentence all over again.

Here's an example:

Brian loves to travel because he loves going places.

Isn't "going places" the same as "travel"? This writer is traveling in circles! A reader still wouldn't know why Brian loves to travel. **A real reason must tell why.**

There is one other kind of reason that is not a reason at all. Instead, it's an **example** of the first part of the sentence. Here's how one might look:

There's a lot of crime in the streets today because criminals are mugging and robbing people.

In this sentence, "mugging" and "robbing" are examples of crime in the streets. They are not the reasons for it. They don't tell why there is so much street crime.

19-2 SKILL BUILDER: RECOGNIZING THE REAL REASON

Some of the sentences below give real reasons for a situation. Some just repeat the first part of the sentence in different words. Still others give examples rather than reasons. Number from 1 to 10 on a sheet of paper. If the sentence does give a real reason, write **RR** next to the matching number. If there is no real reason, rewrite the sentence with a new reason that really tells why.

1. Jack hated Ernie because he couldn't stand the sight of him.
2. The baseball team lost the game because their pitchers were weak.
3. People have accidents in the home because they fall off ladders or cut themselves on sharp knives.
4. The little boy cried because he had scraped his knee.
5. Many TV commercials are annoying because they really get on my nerves.
6. Lots of men and women don't earn enough money at their jobs because they aren't being paid enough.
7. She told everyone lies about me because she was jealous of me.
8. Many marriages are breaking up because people get divorced.
9. Old people have many physical problems because they have poor eyesight and stiff fingers.
10. She was good at sports because she could play golf, tennis, and volleyball well.

Here is an example of a paragraph developed by giving reasons:

Why Big Families Can Be Fun
Clue Word: why

Life in a big family is never lonely. Of course, when you have to take a ticket to get into the bathroom in the morning, a little loneliness would be okay. It would also be okay when you're trying to talk privately on the phone. Not only does the whole family listen to your conversation, but everyone is ready with advice. That's another good thing about big families. You never have to worry about where your next piece of advice is coming from. Furthermore, in a big family, you can always borrow something to wear. In fact, you always need to borrow because someone has already taken your own stuff. In addition, there is always somebody around to blast the stereo when you want to sleep or study. If you grow up in a family like this, you may be bothered, but you'll never be bored.

Drawing by Geo. Price;
© 1974 *The New Yorker Magazine,* Inc.

"About four months ago, he had a room added to the house, and I haven't laid eyes on him since."

Here is an example of a paragraph developed by comparison and contrast:

The City By Day and
The City By Night

Hidden Clue: two views of the city

Night or day, the city is a place that's alive with excitement. In the daytime, people crowd the streets. They are rushing to jobs, homes, stores, and schools. Hustle and bustle are everywhere. Taxis honk, buses roar, and trucks rumble. Litter baskets overflow, and bags of smelly garbage line the sidewalks. When night falls, however, everything changes. The excitement is of a different kind. Now, people are on their way to have a good time. They're not rushing any more. Instead, they are laughing and strolling along. The darkness hides the dirt and the daytime problems. Lights go on everywhere, sparkling like diamonds against the black velvet sky. Cars and buses roll along more quietly. Their headlights light up the night. The tempo slows down, but the action goes on in the city night and day.

Trying It on Your Own

1. Take a good look at this picture.

a. Write a sentence telling what problem this girl might have.

b. Write three sentences telling why she might be reaching out to the house.

c. Write two sentences telling what the results might be if she stays out in the field all night.

d. Write two sentences explaining the ways the girl could convince her family to let her back into the house.

2. Turn back to the Clue Word Chart you filled in at the end of Chapter Twelve. Choose any two of the titles on the chart. Write a complete paragraph for each one. Be sure to:

a. double-check the clue words in your titles

b. note what the clue words tell you to do

c. set up a scribble sheet for each paragraph before you begin to write

3. Look again at page 72. You'll find the following list of titles:

a. Going to School Is the Same As Working At a Job

b. TV Cops and Real-Life Cops

c. City Life Is More Exciting Than Country Life

d. Soccer Is Very Much Like Football

e. Family Life Is Not What It Used to Be

Choose one of these. Then, develop it into a paragraph of comparison and contrast. Don't forget to set up a scribble sheet before you start.

20
Making the Right Connections with Linking Words

What makes a paragraph flow smoothly? One idea links up easily with the next. Writers do this by using **linking words—**words that link—or connect—ideas together.

Think of linking words as traffic signs. When you want to show your reader that you are going on with the idea you started, use:

ALSO
ANOTHER
IN ADDITION
IN FACT
FURTHERMORE

Here's how to use "straight ahead" words.

1. One reason I want to be a nurse is to help people. <u>Another</u> reason is that nurses always find work.
2. Jonelle is the smartest girl in our class. She is <u>also</u> the friendliest.
3. Barry lifts weights and exercises to keep fit. <u>In addition,</u> he jogs three miles a day.
4. Teenagers usually eat too much junk food. <u>Furthermore,</u> they often skip regular meals.

5. Some people think schools have become too easy. <u>In fact,</u> they say students aren't learning to read and write.

When you want to show your reader that you are switching to an opposite idea, use:

HOWEVER
INSTEAD
NEVERTHELESS
ON THE OTHER HAND

Here's how to use "detour" words.

1. My sister was married when she was only 17. <u>However,</u> the marriage didn't last.
2. The chances of winning the lottery are about a million to one. <u>Nevertheless,</u> people keep buying lottery tickets.
3. I thought Tony was going to ask me to the dance. <u>Instead,</u> he invited my best friend.
4. Big-time boxers can make a lot of money. <u>On the other hand,</u> they can get badly hurt in the ring.

When you want to show your reader that you are taking the time to give an example of the point you just made, use:

FOR EXAMPLE
FOR INSTANCE

Here's how to use "slow down" words.

1. Farmers work hard. <u>For example,</u> they have to get up at sunrise to milk their cows.
2. In many ways, the world is getting smaller. <u>For instance,</u> you can fly to Europe now on the fastest jets in about four hours.

ROAD ENDING

When you want to show your reader that you have reached a conclusion based on all the things you have already said, use:

AS A RESULT
THEREFORE

Here's how to use "road ending" words.

1. Many new careers are opening up to women. <u>As a result,</u> young girls growing up today feel they can be anything they want to be.
2. Small children believe everything you tell them. <u>Therefore,</u> you should never lie to them.

Notice that the comma rule you learned about time words is true for linking words, too. Remember the rule? Put a comma after a linking word only when it stands **all by itself** at the beginning of your sentence.

In addition, he jogs three miles a day.
For example, they have to get up at sunrise to milk their cows.
However, the marriage didn't last.
Therefore, you should never lie to them.
BUT
She is also the friendliest.
Another reason is that nurses can always find work.

20-1 SKILL BUILDER: USING LINKING WORDS

For each set of sentences, select one of the words in parentheses to give the correct traffic signal. Then, write each complete set of sentences in your notebook, putting in a comma if it is necessary after the linking word you've chosen.
1. People everywhere want peace. (Nevertheless, In fact) wars seem to break out often in different parts of the world.
2. One reason students enjoy a class is that they like the subject. (Also, Another) reason is that they like the teacher.

3. Thousands of fans buy tickets for the World Series. (In addition, For example) millions more watch the games on TV.
4. Many people have problems caused by air pollution. (On the other hand, For instance) sick or old people often have trouble breathing.
5. To save gas, car makers are building smaller cars. (Also, Instead) they are trying to give buyers better mileage.
6. Most young people love rock music. (However, Furthermore) older people are often not too crazy about it.
7. Life is more pleasant when people are friendly. (Therefore, Nevertheless) we should all be good to one another.
8. Sometimes you think you're getting a real bargain. (For example, Instead) you wind up with a piece of junk.
9. Careful drivers are always alert. (In fact, On the other hand) they never take their eyes off the road.
10. Good citizens take care of their parks and playgrounds. (However, As a result) the parks are beautiful.

Trying It on Your Own

1. Re-read all the sample paragraphs in Chapter Nineteen. In your notebook, write down all the linking words you find in each one. Then, tell what traffic signal each word gives.

2. In the paragraph that follows, use your notebook to fill in each blank with the linking word that best connects one idea to the next.

   People think that tall basketball players have an easy time. _____, this is not true. They have problems like the rest of us. _____, people stare at them when they walk into a room or ride an elevator. _____, they have difficulty finding the right size shoes or clothing. _____, when they fly in planes, they have no comfortable place to put their long legs. _____ inconvenience is that most hotel beds are too short for them. They _____ have trouble walking under most regular-sized doorways. _____, they try to make the best of these things. What really gets to them is a smart remark from a wise guy. _____, people think they're funny when they ask, "How's the weather up there?" Basketball players sometimes hear that line ten times a day. _____, they would really like to tell some people off. _____, they have to be polite to the public. Putting up with all these things is the price they pay for being extra tall. _____, they've learned to accept them.

21
Clinching the Conclusion

The doctor went up to visit the sick woman but came down in a few minutes to ask her husband for a screwdriver. A few minutes later he was down again and asked for a can opener. Still later he was back for a chisel and a hammer. The worried husband couldn't stand it any longer.

"Please tell me what's wrong with my wife, Doc," he cried.

Did you get the joke? Of course not. There's no ending, no punch line. The joke just runs out of steam. It leaves you saying, "So what?"

Now read the joke again—this time with the punch line added.

The doctor went up to visit the sick woman but came down in a few minutes to ask her husband for a screwdriver. A few minutes later he was down again and asked for a can opener. Still later he was back for a chisel and a hammer. The worried husband couldn't stand it any longer.

"Please tell me what's wrong with my wife, Doc," he cried.

"Don't know yet," replied the doctor. "I can't get the lock of my bag open."

The difference is clear. With the ending, you get the point. Without it, you don't.

WRITING A GOOD CONCLUDING SENTENCE

Paragraphs work the same way. They have to have a **concluding sentence.** The concluding sentence is the last sentence in your paragraph. It ties all your ideas and details together. It makes—or clinches—your point. Remember: A good concluding sentence clinches the main idea of your paragraph.

There are four ways to write a good concluding sentence:

1. Tell the idea of your topic sentence in different words.
2. Tell how to change the situation or solve the problem.
3. Tell what might happen if the situation stays the same.
4. Say something that will leave your reader feeling happy or pleased, or sad or angry.

Here, in dark type, are samples of each kind of concluding sentence:

Why People Love Horror Movies

People love going to horror movies. One reason is that they like to be scared by monsters like Frankenstein, Dracula, and the Mummy. People scream in terror at these horrible creatures on the screen. They also enjoy movies about ghosts and haunted houses. They get thrills and chills from watching killer birds, killer rats, and killer sharks. Another reason people keep on crowding into movie theaters is to see demons and devils. They enjoy all these horrors because they know they're not real. It's fun to scream when there is no real danger. **That's probably why we enjoy horror movies so much.**

CONCLUDING SENTENCE
Tells the idea of the topic sentence in different words.

The Problem of Forgetting

Being absent-minded is a problem many people face. They just don't seem to be able to remember things. They forget their keys, umbrellas, and lunches. Sometimes they even forget that they are supposed to meet someone. This kind of forgetting can be a real pain in the neck. Absent-minded people waste their own time and annoy other people. They are always explaining why they were late or why they never showed up at all. Their friends get tired of hearing their excuses. **The easiest way to solve this problem is to keep a daily diary and check it every day.**

CONCLUDING SENTENCE
Tells how to change the situation or solve the problem.

The Effects of Modern Life in Africa

As Africa becomes more modern, the wild animals there face great danger. One effect of modern life is that people need more and more land. They have to build cities. They have to build factories. Another effect is that they must have railroads, highways, and airports. To get these things, people have to push deeper and deeper into the jungle. Therefore, the animals are losing their water supplies. They also can't find enough food. Whole herds of these wild animals are dying out. **Unless something is done immediately to protect them, the beautiful animals of Africa will no longer exist.**

Blue Jeans of Yesterday and Today

Jeans are the most popular clothes in the world. This was not always so. Years ago, only farmers and workers wore them. Then, teenagers discovered them. They didn't want the uptight, buttoned-down look of the older generation. They wanted a free and easy way of dressing. Today, people of all ages are copying the kids. Everybody's into jeans. Even glamorous movie stars and models wear them. Instead of being work clothes, jeans have become high-fashion clothes. Teenagers can be mighty proud of themselves. **They knew a good thing when they saw one.**

Very often, the same paragraph can be ended with any of the four different kinds of concluding sentences. It all depends on the point you want to clinch.

The picture on the next page, for example, might give you many ideas for a paragraph about the way numbers rule our lives today. Our names are no longer important. Instead, we're known by our social security numbers, bank account numbers, credit card numbers, and so on.

If you wanted to restate the main idea in different words, your concluding sentence could be:

> As modern life becomes more complicated, we will need to rely more and more on these numbers.

If you wanted to tell how to change the situation, your concluding sentence could be:

> We must insist on our right to be treated as human beings and not just as numbers!

CONCLUDING SENTENCE
Tells what might happen if the situation stays the same.

CONCLUDING SENTENCE
Says something that leaves the reader feeling pleased.

116

If you wanted to tell what might happen if the situation continues, your concluding sentence could be:

> If things keep up this way, babies will be given numbers instead of names when they're born.

If you wanted to say something that would leave your reader feeling sad, your concluding sentence could be:

> It's just too bad that we live in a world where numbers are more important than people.

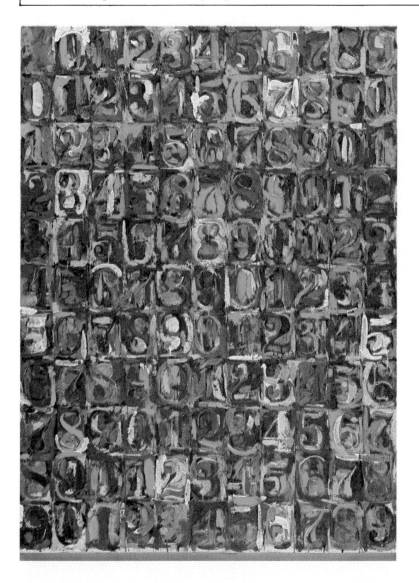

21-1
SKILL BUILDER:
CHOOSING
THE RIGHT CONCLUDING
SENTENCE

You try it now. Answer the question that follows each of these paragraphs and write the right concluding sentence in your notebook.

A. All over the country, school cafeterias are changing. The people in charge finally realized that most students hated the food being served. Millions of dollars were being wasted. Some kids refused to eat cafeteria food at all. Others took a few bites and threw the rest away. Finally, one school out West got the idea of serving hamburgers, shakes, and fries. Business boomed. The students in that school were getting the kinds of food they liked. Other schools quickly got the idea. They even added things like pizza and hero sandwiches to the menu. _____.

Concluding Sentence Choices: Which one tells what might happen if the situation stays the same?
1. School cafeterias are not what they used to be.
2. To be healthy, young people should learn to eat foods that are good for them.
3. If this trend continues, school cafeterias will be the greatest places in town to eat.
4. Hamburgers are America's most popular food.

B. People often misunderstand each other. They only listen to the words the other person speaks. However, we all use more than words to get across our messages. One way we show our feelings is by the tone of our voices. A loud voice can express anger or annoyance. A soft voice can show love or tenderness. Another way we show how we feel is with body language. We raise our eyebrows to show we are surprised. We tap our toes or fingers when we are nervous. We turn away when we are bored. _____.

Concluding Sentence Choices: Which one tells how to change the situation or solve the problem?

1. Therefore, to understand others, we should watch what they do as well as listen to what they say.
2. Experts say that 55 percent of what we tell other people about ourselves isn't said in words at all.
3. If we all keep using body language and voice tone, we may stop using words altogether.
4. People often act just plain silly when they're talking.

C. Each year innocent animals suffer from the effects of cruel laboratory experiments. Rabbits, mice, and guinea pigs are used to test perfumes, make-up, and hair dyes. Powders are blown into their eyes until they go blind. In addition, they are forced to breathe chemicals that make them terribly sick or even drive them crazy. Other chemicals are injected right into their blood to see how much would be safe for humans to take. The animals suffer for weeks until they finally die. All this is done so the big cosmetic companies can have more and more products to sell. _____ _____.

Concluding Sentence Choices: Which one leaves the reader feeling sad or angry?

1. Many people are trying to stop these animal experiments.
2. Every time you buy one of those products, you should think of the helpless animal that gave its life for you.
3. As the experiments go on, more and more cosmetic products will be developed.
4. Laboratories should be kept cleaner and safer.

D. Teenagers have many reasons for joining clubs. One reason is that a club is a place to meet new people and make new friends. Planning and doing things together makes it easier to feel comfortable with the other people in the group. Another reason is that club members are usually interested in the same activities. It's more fun to share sports or hobbies with other young people who enjoy doing the same things. A third reason teenagers join clubs is that being part of a group makes them feel good about themselves. They have a feeling of belonging. _____.

Concluding Sentence Choices: Which tells the idea of the topic sentence?

1. There are more clubs today than ever before.
2. Getting into a club is not easy.
3. If teenagers join clubs, they'll never learn to get along on their own.
4. Joining a club meets many teenage needs.

Trying It on Your Own

1. Imagine that you have only one day to spend in the country. The picture shows you all the things you can enjoy there. You'd love to do every one, but you don't have enough time. Write a concluding sentence to a paragraph that explains how you would solve the problem of which activities to choose.

2. Imagine you have a job in a summer resort, but you are not allowed to do any of the things the picture shows. Only paying guests can use the pool, the tennis courts, and all the other sports facilities. You, as a worker, are forbidden to go near them. Write a concluding sentence that tells what might happen if this situation continues or stays the same.

3. Now, imagine you have a whole summer at a resort. All the facilities are yours to use. You are free to have all the fun you can. Write a concluding sentence that would leave your reader feeling as happy about it as you are.

4. Imagine you have to write a paragraph about your wonderful summer that starts with this topic sentence:

   Every city kid should get at least one chance to spend a summer in the country.

   Write a concluding sentence for a paragraph like this that re-tells the topic sentence in different words.

Putting It All Together 22

By now, you've built up a powerhouse of writing skills. You know how to get started with a scribble sheet. You know what paragraph unity means. You know what makes a good topic sentence and a good concluding sentence. You know you have to use sensory words and action words to open up your details. You know all about clue words, time words, and linking words, too.

You can tell a story. You can write a description. You can explain your ideas or feelings in five different ways. You can write!

Here's your chance to turn all that power on full blast.

When we think about children's lives, we tend to think only of the happy moments. However, children are often unhappy and afraid. The picture on page 122 shows that clearly. Children are small, and everyone else is big. Life can be full of terrors and dangers to them.

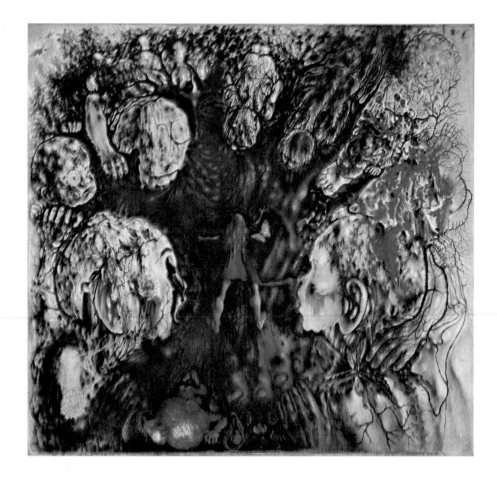

1. Write a story about something bad that happened to you in your own childhood.
2. Write a description of a person or a place that scared you when you were a child.
3. Write a paragraph telling the effects of spoiling a child.
4. Write a paragraph telling the problems of growing up without a father or without a mother.
5. Write a paragraph comparing the fears of children with the fears of grown-ups.
6. Write a paragraph telling the ways children can hurt or disappoint their parents.
7. Write a paragraph telling why you would not want to be a young child again.

23
Making Your Opinions Count

Writing is a wonderful way of finding out who you really are and what you really think. All the skills you have been practicing in this book can help you to do just that. Instead of settling for only your first idea, you've been learning how to think things through.

Recognizing that you have opinions of your own is part of growing up. In life, there are many situations which force you to make a decision for yourself. Sometimes you have to advise someone else about what to do. Other times you have to sort out your own feelings before you can decide what your opinion really is. Writing it out keeps you focused on the problem. You're not influenced by other people. It's what *you* think and what *you* say that count.

Having friends and being part of a group is very important. However, many young people have been hurt by going along too far with the crowd. How important is your crowd to you? Could there be a time when you would not go along with what they do?

23-1
SKILL BUILDER: MAKING A DECISION

Read each of the situations explained below. Then, write a paragraph for each one, telling what you would do and why you would do it. A scribble sheet will help you to get your thoughts together. Your topic sentence should refer to the situation you are discussing.

1. You and a friend are strolling through a department store. Your friend says she's going to steal some clothing "just for fun." You don't like the idea, and you tell her so. She calls you "chicken" and says it's easy to get away with it. Before you know it, she has grabbed some blouses from a table and is running out of the store. You start to run, too, but a store detective grabs you. Your friend has gotten away. Now, the detective tells you that he will call the police if you don't tell him your friend's name and address. He will have you arrested as an accomplice to the theft. You could be in serious trouble. What do you do?

2a. You are a girl who has agreed to go to a big dance with a boy who is just okay. He's nothing special. Two days before the dance, a really super guy you just met asks you to go out with him on the same night as the dance is being held. What do you do?

2b. You are a boy who has asked a girl to a big dance, and she has accepted. Two days before the dance, she calls you to say she can't go. She tells you something important has come up, but you don't believe her. What do you do?

3. You are in line for a nice promotion on your after-school job. As a result of a misunderstanding, however, your boss thinks that something you said to him was rude. You didn't mean it the way he took it. Nevertheless, he won't accept your explanation. He insists on an apology. You don't think you should apologize for something you really didn't say. However, you will probably lose out on that promotion if you don't give the boss an apology. What do you do?

23-2 SKILL BUILDER: GIVING GOOD ADVICE

You've seen advice columns in the newspapers many times. Here's a chance to try your own hand at it. Consider carefully each of the problems explained in the letters. Then, write a letter in your notebook that tells that person how to handle the problem. Follow the letter form shown and address the answer to the name signed by the letter writer.

Dear Jody Hall,

I'm not too good-looking. I don't have the money for sharp clothes. I'm not too good at most sports. On account of this, I don't have any friends. What should I do?

Sincerely,
Lonely Guy

Dear Jody Hall,

My twin sister goes with a guy I really dig. I'm really crazy about him. I think I could get him away from her, but I don't want to hurt my sister's feelings. What should I do?

Sincerely,
Troubled Twin

Dear Jody Hall:

I have two best friends. I like them both very much, but they hate each other. I don't want to stay with just one of them. The problem is whenever we get together, they always fight. What should I do?

Sincerely,
Miserable

23-3 SKILL BUILDER: TAKING SIDES

When there are two sides to a question, you have to think through your own feelings before you can decide which side you're on. Read each of the following paragraphs carefully. Decide how you feel. Then, take either A or B as your topic sentence and develop it into a paragraph of your own, giving your reasons for taking that side.

1. You need a license to do almost anything. You need a license to hunt or fish. You need a license to sell liquor or to run a beauty parlor. You need a license to drive a car, and you need a license to get married. However, for one of the most important things of all, no license is needed. You don't need a license to be a parent. Anyone may raise a child. No training or experience is required. No proof of ability is needed.
   A. All adults should be required to get a parent's license before they can bring children into the world.
   B. Having children is a very private matter, and no license should be required to be a parent.

2. Today, doctors can keep people alive for a long time with machines. They can do this even when they know there's no hope that the patient will ever get better. The person may be in great pain. Sometimes the person stays unconscious for months, even years. All kinds of needles, tubes, and wires are attached to the patient's body. The person is almost more like a machine than a human being.
   A. When there is no hope for recovery, people should be allowed to die in peace.
   B. No matter how hopeless it seems, doctors should fight to keep a person alive any way they can.

3. More and more, the government seems to be telling people what they should or should not eat. A few years ago, government scientists stopped the sale of any foods that contained cyclamates. Cyclamates are chemicals that were used in diet foods as a substitute for sugar. The scientists said that cyclamates were harmful to health. Naturally, people who used diet foods and sodas were very unhappy. Since then, the government has named other harmful chemicals in our foods. They want to ban these foods, too.
   A. The government should not interfere with people's right to buy the foods they want.
   B. The government has the responsibility to prevent the sale of harmful foods.

23-4 SKILL BUILDER: MAKING CHOICES

When you have to choose only one thing out of several that you value, you have to think about your feelings pretty carefully. What do you value most? Read each of following problems. Think about them. Then, in your notebook, write each of the paragraphs called for to explain the choice you would make.

1. Five people are dying of a rare and terrible disease. The doctors have finally come up with the only medicine that can cure it. However, right now they have only enough to save one person. If you had to choose, which one of the following people would you save? Write a paragraph telling which person you choose. Tell why you choose that person.

PEOPLE:

a. Male, age 23. Star quarterback. Spends summers teaching football to poor city kids to give them same chance he got.

b. Female, age 15. Only child in family. Sweet, pleasant, has many friends. Plans to be a nurse and works hard in school.

c. Male, age 36. Extremely rich, has given millions of dollars to charity. Now says if he gets the medicine, he'll build a special clinic for people who get this disease in the future.

d. Male, age 42. Has five kids, aged 4 to 12. No wife or other relatives. Works two jobs to keep family together. If he dies, kids will have to go to foster homes or orphan asylum.

e. Female, age 56. Brilliant scientist. Has made many important medical discoveries. When she got sick, she was working on a cure for cancer.

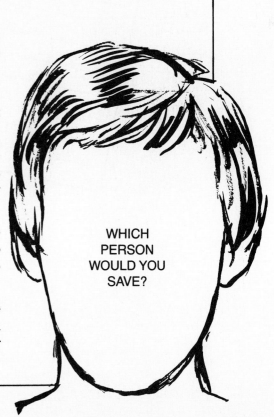

WHICH PERSON WOULD YOU SAVE?

2. You have your pick of two summer jobs. The first sounds like a lot of fun, but it has no future. The second job has a future, but doesn't sound like much fun. They both pay about the same. Which job would you take? Write a paragraph telling which job you would choose. Tell why you choose that job.

JOB NO. 1:

You have a chance for a summer job at a record company. You'll only run errands and go for coffee. However, you'll get to meet many rock groups. You'll see records being cut. You may even get invited to a big party or two.

JOB NO. 2:

At the same time, you also have a chance for a summer job as a cashier in a department store. If you do well, they'll give you a part-time job as a salesperson when school starts. Then, after you graduate, the job will become a full-time one.

3. You've promised your kid sister to go with her to her first dance. She really wants to go, but she's nervous because she's never been to a dance before. She's counting on you to be there to help her get over her shyness. On the day of the dance, however, your friend telephones you, all excited. By some miracle, your friend has managed to get two tickets to a sold-out performance of your favorite rock group. It's a one-night-only concert, and it's tonight—the night of the dance. You have to choose between keeping your promise to your sister and going to the concert. Write a paragraph telling where you would choose to go. Tell why you make that choice.

SISTER:
She's really looking forward to the dance, but you know she won't go without you. You gave her your word, and she's depending on you.

CONCERT:
This is your one-time-only chance to see and hear this great rock group in person. You have all their albums, but you know that hearing their music on records can never match the excitement of a live performance.

BIG DANCE!
3 — BANDS — 3
SATURDAY NIGHT
8:30 P.M.
LIVE MUSIC
DANCE! DANCE!

H 2 cu
CONCERT
SATURDAY
NIGHT
8:30 P.M.
H 2 cu
CONCERT

Trying It on Your Own

1. Are you willing to be laughed at or left out? Write a paragraph telling when—if ever—you would refuse to go along with what your crowd is doing. Would you refuse even if it meant that you wouldn't have any more friends?

2.   Old age can be a difficult time. Old people often don't have much money. Sometimes, they are not well. Frequently, they are lonely. Many people think this is wrong. They say we should all

help the elderly and be kind to them. Often, however, it's easy to say these things and not so easy to do them. Write a paragraph telling what you would do if you were asked to volunteer your Saturday afternoons to visit with the old people at a senior citizen center. Would you be willing to give up other things you'd rather do with your Saturdays?

24
Building Up Your Sentence Power

There is one more very important kind of sentence combining you need to know about. This is something you **must** do in order to avoid making sentence errors. Without it, you won't have even two short, choppy sentences. Instead, you will be left with one complete sentence and only a part of another. Here is how it works.

Now look at—and listen to—the differences between the "before" and "after" sentences:

---

1. BEFORE: Unless you clean your room.
   You won't be allowed to go out this weekend.
   AFTER: Unless you clean your room, you won't be allowed to go out this weekend.

---

2. BEFORE: When my friends want to have a party.
   I'm always ready to join in.
   AFTER: When my friends want to have a party, I'm always ready to join in.

---

3. BEFORE: If it rains tomorrow.
   Our picnic will be called off.
   AFTER: If it rains tomorrow, our picnic will be called off.

You can see that in each case, the first sentence is not complete. It leaves you hanging. You don't find out what will happen until you get to the second sentence. To correct this, you have to join the two parts into one long, strong sentence. This is how it's done:

1. LEARN THESE 15 WORDS BY HEART. THEY ARE WORDS THAT CAN LEAVE A SENTENCE HANGING. HERE'S A TRICK THAT WILL HELP YOU REMEMBER ALL THE WORDS: JUST THINK OF "A WHITE BUS."

A   after, although

W   when, which, while

H   how

I   if

T   that

E   even though

B   because, before

U   unless, until

S   since, so that

2. WHEN YOUR FIRST SENTENCE BEGINS WITH ANY ONE OF THESE HANGING WORDS, CHANGE THE PERIOD AT THE END OF THE SENTENCE TO A COMMA.

3. CHANGE THE CAPITAL LETTER THAT BEGINS THE SECOND SENTENCE TO A SMALL LETTER (UNLESS THE BEGINNING WORD IS SOMEBODY'S NAME). THEN, ADD ON THE SECOND SENTENCE TO SENTENCE NUMBER ONE.

SENTENCE COMBINING TO MAKE YOUR SENTENCES COMPLETE

Follow these three steps to combine each of the following pairs of sentences into one long, strong, and complete sentence.

1. Although they did their best.
   The team lost anyway.
2. If you run as fast as you can.
   You might catch the bus.
3. Because I've been eating too much.
   I've gained a lot of weight.
4. Until she saw the price.
   She planned to buy the stereo.
5. While I was washing my hair.
   The phone rang.
6. Since we didn't have enough money for carfare.
   We had to walk home.
7. After I read the book.
   I could hardly wait to see the movie.
8. Before you can apply for a job.
   You have to get working papers.
9. Unless a soda is ice cold.
   I won't drink it.
10. When dad left the kitchen.
    The dog gobbled up all the hamburgers.

It's even easier to build complete sentences, the way you just did, when it's the second sentence in a pair that starts out with one of the hanging words. Now look at—and listen to—the differences between these "before" and "after" sentences.

---

1. BEFORE: She bet on the horse.
   Which came in last.
   AFTER: She bet on the horse which came in last.

---

2. BEFORE: Phil won the prize.
   That everyone else wanted.
   AFTER: Phil won the prize that everyone else wanted.

---

3. BEFORE: The kids went to the beach.
   Because it was such a hot day.
   AFTER: The kids went to the beach because it was such a hot day.

You can see that in each of these cases, the second sentence is the one that's not complete. To make the correction, you have to join the two sentences together once again. This is how it's done:

---

1. DOUBLE-CHECK THE HANGING WORDS:

   A after, although

   W when, which, while
   H how
   I if
   T that
   E even though

   B because, before
   U unless, until
   S since, so that

2. DROP THE PERIOD AT THE END OF THE FIRST SENTENCE.
3. CHANGE THE CAPITAL LETTER THAT BEGINS THE SECOND SENTENCE TO A SMALL LETTER. THEN, ADD ON THE SECOND SENTENCE TO SENTENCE NUMBER ONE.

24-2 SKILL BUILDER:

MORE SENTENCE COMBINING TO MAKE YOUR SENTENCES COMPLETE

Follow these three steps to combine each of the following pairs of sentences into one long, strong, and complete sentence.

1. Tom hit a home run.
   Which won the game for us.
2. You can't play the guitar well.
   Unless you practice regularly.
3. I missed the special TV program.
   That everyone is talking about.
4. She completed her homework assignment.
   While she was in the library.
5. We won't have any hot water.
   Until the boiler is fixed.
6. She took a class in water safety.
   So that she could learn to be a lifeguard.
7. Douglas bought the leather coat he wanted.
   Even though it was expensive.
8. I got soaked in the rain.
   Because I forgot my umbrella.
9. They could do it.
   If they really wanted to.
10. We always cook a special dinner.
    When my aunt comes to visit.

Trying It on Your Own

Below is a paragraph that contains both complete sentences and incomplete sentences. All the incomplete sentences begin with hanging words. They have to be combined with either the sentence that goes before or the sentence that comes after. Read the story carefully to see which sentences should go together. Then, rewrite the paragraph according to the sentence combining methods you've learned in this chapter.

A Surprise Party

Even though my brother didn't know it. I was planning a birthday party for him. So that he wouldn't guess what I was doing. I didn't even say a word about his birthday. I telephoned all his friends. While he was out of the house. I couldn't really imagine. How they would all keep the secret. If anyone gave a hint to my brother. The whole surprise would be ruined. I was nervous and excited. When the night of the party finally arrived. Before I could decorate the house and fix the food. I had to wait for my brother to leave the house. Because they wanted to be there for the surprise. All his friends arrived on time. When my brother opened the door. We all jumped out and yelled, "Surprise!" After my brother got over the shock. He said the party was the best birthday present I had ever given him.

25
Knowing When To Stop a Sentence

Now that you know as much as you do about building long, strong, and complete sentences, there is one last word to be said. The word is **run-on**. A run-on is a sentence that goes on . . . and on . . . and on. . . . We do want to combine short, choppy sentences into long ones, of course. What we *don't* want are sentences that don't know when to stop.

Try reading this sentence out loud without pausing to take a breath:

My mother works two jobs to make as much money as she can she says she won't take a vacation until all her kids have finished school.

Quite a mouthful, isn't it? The real problem, though, is that it isn't really a sentence at all. It's two sentences run together without a stop.

Read it this way now:

My mother works two jobs to make as much money as she can. She says she won't take a vacation until all her kids have finished school.

The period after "can" shows where the first complete idea ends. The period after "school" shows where the second complete

138

idea ends. This is always one sure way to get rid of run-ons.

> **CORRECT A RUN-ON SENTENCE BY PUTTING A PERIOD AFTER EACH COMPLETE IDEA.**

A second way to get rid of run-ons is to use a comma plus one of five connecting words. Two of the words are your old friends **and** and **but**. The other three are **or, so,** and **yet.** These five words always go in the middle of a sentence. They aren't used to start a sentence. Any one of them, together with a comma, can build a bridge between two complete ideas. The comma can't do it alone. Add one of the connecting words as well. Here's how they work:

---

1. RUN-ON: There's a rock concert in the park tonight, I wouldn't miss it for anything.

   CORRECT: There's a rock concert in the park tonight, and I wouldn't miss it for anything.

---

2. RUN-ON: I was supposed to go shopping with my sister, I'd rather hear music than buy clothes.

   CORRECT: I was supposed to go shopping with my sister, but I'd rather hear music than buy clothes.

---

3. RUN-ON: Dinner has to be served early tonight, I'll never get out of my house in time otherwise.

   CORRECT: Dinner has to be served early tonight, or I'll never get out of my house in time otherwise.

---

4. RUN-ON: They expect about a thousand people at the concert, I want to be there early to get a seat.

   CORRECT: They expect about a thousand people at the concert, so I want to be there early to get a seat.

---

5. RUN-ON: They're supposed to stop selling tickets when all the seats are taken, at every concert there are always people who are left standing.

   CORRECT: They're supposed to stop selling tickets when all the seats are taken, yet at every concert there are always people who are left standing.

25-1 SKILL BUILDER:

CORRECTING
RUN-ON SENTENCES

Rewrite each of the following run-on sentences. Use a period, or a comma plus a connecting word, to correct each one.

1. Traveling can be a lot of fun many people enjoy going to different places every year.
2. Some like to visit different parts of our own country, others like to visit foreign countries.
3. You can go to faraway vacation places where you can see great mountains and oceans, you can go to big cities where you can see famous museums and churches.
4. Usually, you want to go somewhere that is different from your own home town you can have a complete change of scene.
5. If you have relatives who live in other states or countries, you are lucky you can always go to visit them.
6. Your relatives will probably want to show you all the sights you may prefer to do things on your own.
7. Travel can give you a chance to learn new things it can just give you a chance to relax.
8. Going away is always exciting, coming home can be a good feeling, too.

Trying It on Your Own

Here is a paragraph that really isn't a paragraph at all. It's written as though it were all one sentence. Read the lines very carefully to figure out the meaning. Then, rewrite the paragraph. Use periods to show where one complete idea ends and the next one begins. Use commas plus connecting words to show that two ideas belong together. Be sure to begin each new sentence with a capital letter.

Why Everyone Loves An Amusement Park

Amusement parks are great fun for people of all ages younger children love the merry-go-round older ones enjoy the faster, more exciting rides teenagers go for the really big attractions like the roller coaster and the ferris wheel everyone tries the games of chance only a few people win the prizes everyone has a good time anyway families can bring picnic lunches they can buy all kinds of delicious foods at the park they can eat red-hot, sizzling frankfurters they can eat juicy hamburgers covered with pickles and relish sometimes there are bands playing in different parts of the park the air is filled with music people dance for hours they don't get tired the crowds stroll around until late at night the lights on all the booths and rides make the amusement park a wonderland of color and fun.

26
Expanding Your Paragraph Power

You know now that a unit paragraph can do it all. It can tell a story, give a description, and explain ideas and feelings. Sometimes, though, you may be asked to write a longer composition. Other times, you might want to try a longer one on your own. That often happens when you find you have a whole lot of separate details to back up your main idea. There's no problem. Now that you can write a solid unit paragraph, you can also write a long composition.

When we talk about a long composition, we mean one that is made up of:

1. an introductory paragraph
2. two or more middle paragraphs
3. a concluding paragraph

By adding two or three sentences to your original topic sentence, you create your introductory paragraph. By building up two or more of your groups of supporting details, you develop your middle paragraphs. By opening up your concluding sentence a bit, you write your concluding paragraph. What makes it all possible is the **scribble sheet**.

In Chapter Six, you had some fun with opening up details about the circus. If those circus details had been written down in scribble sheet form, they could have looked like this:

I Love the Circus

circus acts

Lots of acts - don't know what to look at first
trapeze artists - fly through the air
animals - elephants
running horses
clowns running and falling music
big red noses spotlights
silly tricks sequins

Costumes

lion tamer
lions and tigers fantastic costumes
dangerous bright colors red purple
silver

Food

voices smells
hot dogs mustard showgirls furs
peanuts soda feathers
popcorn satin
cotton candy

Grouping the scribble sheet details shows us that we have the most to say about three things: the circus acts, the beautiful costumes, and the delicious food. As we saw once before, in Chapter Ten, all three groups support the one main idea of why people love to visit the circus.

Here, then, is a unit paragraph that we might develop from the circus scribble sheet:

I Love the Circus

All the things I see and do at a circus are super. First, there are the fantastic costumes. Red, purple, and silver sequins glitter in the spotlight. Gleaming and shimmering, the costumes dazzle my eyes. Next, there are the acts that scare me or make me laugh. If the trapeze artists miss by one second, they can crash to the ground. The lion tamer, who could be attacked at any minute, cracks the whip at the snarling lions and tigers. When the funny clowns come tumbling in, their big red noses and silly tricks make me laugh. While all this is going on, I eat myself silly. I gobble up crunchy peanuts and popcorn. I munch on spicy hot dogs. I even finish off a whole cone of gooey cotton candy. In between, I wash everything down with cups of cold, fizzy soda. I've been going to the circus since I was a little kid, and I still love it.

EXPANDING THE TOPIC SENTENCE INTO AN INTRODUCTORY PARAGRAPH

An introductory paragraph needs at least three sentences. Your first sentence is still your topic sentence—the one that's like an umbrella. It has to cover all the scribble sheet details you plan to include in your composition. The other sentences—the ones in dark type below—in your introductory paragraph tell your reader what your main scribble sheet groupings are. In other words, they prepare your reader for the composition that follows.

TOPIC SENTENCE	INTRODUCTORY PARAGRAPH
All the things I see and do at a circus are super.	All the things I see and do at a circus are super. **The costumes are beautiful. The acts are exciting. The food is delicious.**

EXPANDING THE SUPPORTING DETAILS INTO BODY PARAGRAPHS

Each middle paragraph in a long composition must have at least six sentences. Each of these paragraphs is based on a different group of details. If you have two big groups of details on your scribble sheet, you need two middle paragraphs. If you have three groups, you need three middle paragraphs. No matter how many there are, these middle paragraphs are usually called the body of your composition.

You develop each one of these body paragraphs by opening up the details as much as you can. The dark type in the body paragraphs below shows you how to open up those details. Tell even more about everything than you would in the unit paragraph. Use all the sensory words and all the action words you can think of. Use all the sentence-combining tools you have learned to make long, strong sentences.

First, there are the fantastic costumes. Red, purple, and silver sequins glitter in the spotlight. Gleaming and shimmering, the costumes dazzle my eyes. Next, there are the acts that scare me or make me laugh. If the trapeze artists miss by one second, they can crash to the ground. The lion tamer, who could be attacked at any minute, cracks the whip at the snarling lions and tigers. When the funny clowns come tumbling in, their big red noses and silly tricks make me laugh. While all this is going on, I eat myself silly. I gobble up crunchy peanuts and popcorn. I munch on spicy hot dogs. I even finish off a whole cone of gooey cotton candy. In between, I wash everything down with cups of cold, fizzy soda.

First, there are the fantastic costumes. Red, purple, and silver sequins glitter in the spotlight. Gleaming and shimmering, the costumes dazzle my eyes. **Some of the performers wear sky-high headdresses of feathers and jewels. The other circus performers march in with capes of glistening satin and rich fur swirling around them. Even the bright red uniforms of the band musicians look terrific.**

Next, there are the acts that scare me or make me laugh. **The trapeze acts risk their lives hundreds of feet above the ground. Twisting and tumbling, they catch each other in mid-air.** If the trapeze artists miss by one second, they can crash to the ground. **The animal acts can also be scary.** The lion tamer, who could be attacked at any minute, cracks the whip at the snarling lions and tigers. When the funny clowns come tumbling in, their big red noses and silly tricks make me laugh. **They throw pies and squirt water all over the place. They keep slipping and sliding and falling.**

While all this is going on, I eat myself silly. I gobble up crunchy peanuts and popcorn. I munch on spicy hot dogs, **dripping with golden yellow mustard.** I even finish off a whole cone of gooey cotton candy. **Sweet and sticky, it melts in my mouth.** In between, I wash everything down with cups of cold, fizzy soda.

EXPANDING THE CONCLUDING SENTENCE INTO A CONCLUDING PARAGRAPH

A concluding paragraph has to have at least two sentences. Three are even better. A concluding paragraph works exactly the same way as a concluding sentence does. It ties all your ideas together in the same four ways as before.

This is what a good concluding paragraph does:

1. It tells the idea of your introductory paragraph in different words.

OR

2. It tells how to change the situation or solve the problem.

OR

3. It tells what might happen if the situation stays the same.

OR

4. It says something that leaves your reader feeling happy or pleased, or sad or angry.

In a unit paragraph, you can do any of these things in one sentence because that sentence is the last line of the total paragraph. In a longer composition, the conclusion must be a separate paragraph. One sentence alone is not a paragraph. Therefore, you need to write two or more sentences to make up a concluding paragraph. The sentences in dark type below show you how to expand a concluding sentence into a concluding paragraph.

CONCLUDING SENTENCE	CONCLUDING PARAGRAPH
I've been going to the circus since I was a little kid, and I still love it.	I've been going to the circus since I was a little kid, and I still love it. **I still laugh at the clowns and get a thrill from the dangerous acts. I still enjoy looking at the fabulous costumes and eating the fun foods.**

Two versions of "I Love the Circus" follow. On the left is the unit paragraph. On the right is the complete five-paragraph composition. Looking at them side by side, you can clearly see how the long composition grew directly out of the unit paragraph. Again, the dark type shows you how the composition was expanded from the unit paragraph.

UNIT PARAGRAPH	LONG COMPOSITION
I Love the Circus	I Love the Circus
All the things I see and do at a circus are super. First, there are the fantastic costumes. Red, purple, and silver sequins glitter in the spotlight. Gleaming and shimmering, the costumes dazzle my eyes. Next, there are the acts that scare me or make me laugh. If the trapeze artists miss by one second, they can crash to the ground. The lion tamer, who could be attacked at any minute, cracks the whip at the snarling lions and tigers. When the funny clowns come tumbling in, their big red noses and silly tricks make me	All the things I see and do at a circus are super. **The costumes are beautiful. The acts are exciting. The food is delicious.** First, there are the fantastic costumes. Red, purple, and silver sequins glitter in the spotlight. Gleaming and shimmering, the costumes dazzle my eyes. **Some of the performers wear sky-high head-dresses of feathers and jewels. The other circus performers march in with capes of glistening satin and rich fur swirling around them. Even the bright red uniforms of the band musicians look terrific.**

laugh. While all this is going on, I eat myself silly. I gobble up crunchy peanuts and popcorn. I munch on spicy hot dogs. I even finish off a whole cone of gooey cotton candy. In between, I wash everything down with cups of cold, fizzy soda. I've been going to the circus since I was a little kid, and I still love it.

Next, there are the acts that scare me or make me laugh. **The trapeze acts risk their lives hundreds of feet above the ground. Twisting and tumbling, they catch each other in mid-air.** If the trapeze artists miss by one second, they can crash to the ground. **The animal acts can also be scary.** The lion tamer, who could be attacked at any minute, cracks the whip at the snarling lions and tigers. When the funny clowns come tumbling in, their big red noses and silly tricks make me laugh. **They throw pies and squirt water all over the place. They keep slipping and sliding and falling down.**

While all this is going on, I eat myself silly. I gobble up crunchy peanuts and popcorn. I munch on spicy hot dogs, **dripping with golden yellow mustard.** I even finish off a whole cone of gooey cotton candy. **Sweet and sticky, it melts in my mouth.** In between, I wash everything down with cups of cold, fizzy soda.

I've been going to the circus since I was a little kid, and I still love it. **I still laugh at the clowns and get a thrill from the dangerous acts. I still enjoy looking at the fabulous costumes and eating the fun foods.**

26-1
SKILL BUILDER:
WRITING THE
LONG COMPOSITION

Here is another scribble sheet and another unit paragraph. Notice that all the details on the scribble sheet have not been used in the unit paragraph. What other details can you add? How can you open up all the details? Decide what more you can say about everything. Then, expand the unit paragraph into a four-paragraph composition entitled "Why People Are Superstitious."

This picture suggests some of the magic signs and symbols that people once believed in. It may give you some more ideas about modern superstitions.

What other people do

What people do themselves

Why People Are Superstitious
Brought-up that way
Everybody has some superstitions
Carry good luck charms
rabbit's foot
lucky penny
horseshoe
four leaf clover
Friday the 13th
Knock on wood
Don't step on a crack
Don't break a mirror
Don't walk under a ladder
Don't let a black cat cross your path

Family's ideas
Read about superstitions
start their own superstitions
clothes bring luck
Job - school
Pass a test
Athletes batter gets a hit
Football player has lucky uniform number
Eating certain foods for luck
Doing things a certain way is lucky

Why People Are Superstitious

Even in this modern age, many people are superstitious. One reason people believe in superstitions is that everyone they know believes in them too. For example, they see their friends carrying good luck charms and knocking on wood to keep away bad luck. They hear about unlucky Friday the 13th. They know that a broken mirror brings bad luck since everybody tells them that it does. Another reason people are superstitious is that certain things have happened to them. Because of these things, they start some private superstitions of their own. For instance, a student may have passed a test on a day she was wearing a red shirt. As a result, she wears that red shirt now every time she has a test. A baseball player might have hit a home run one day when he was chewing tobacco. Now, he never steps up to the plate without a wad of tobacco in his mouth. If people get too serious about it all, superstition can start to run their lives.

How did your composition turn out? Did you follow all the steps? Did you expand your topic sentence, your supporting details, your concluding sentence? In case you missed something, let's go through the steps one more time. This time, we'll take the title "How Lottery Winners Get Fooled." Here's our scribble sheet:

How Lottery Winners Get Fooled

Government takes big chunk of the money

Everybody thinks you're rich — wants things

Money not paid —

All at once

People keep calling

Write you letters

Not as much money as you think

Jealous of you

not fair

Fear of getting robbed

Argument in family

No more privacy

Lots of expenses

People stare and point at you

Relatives get nasty

Talk about you

Friends get angry

Don't know what to do first

Don't get money you expect

Trouble with family and friends

Again, the dark type shows you how the unit paragraph is expanded into a long composition.

151

UNIT PARAGRAPH
How Lottery Winners Get Fooled

Winning the lottery isn't all it's cracked up to be. First of all, the government grabs more than half your winnings. You never even get your hands on that part of the money. When you buy the ticket, they promise you as much as a million dollars, but it isn't true. Another way you get fooled is by trusting your relatives and friends. You think they will all be happy for you. If you don't give it, you suddenly find yourself all alone. It's no fun to wind up with a little money and a lot of grief.

LONG COMPOSITION
How Lottery Winners Get Fooled

Winning the lottery isn't all it's cracked up to be. **You don't get as much money as you think you'll get. Your family and your friends can turn nasty.**

First of all, the government grabs more than half your winnings. **It's a very unfair system. The way it works is that the government takes its share right up front. However, you don't get your part all at one time. Instead, you only get a certain amount of it each year.** When you buy the ticket, they promise you as much as a million dollars, but it isn't true.

Another way you get fooled is by trusting your relatives and friends. You think they will all be happy for you. **However, everybody asks you for something. Cousins, aunts, and uncles you haven't heard from in ten years suddenly come to visit. Your friends think you ought to buy them clothes, stereos, and whatever else they want.** If you don't give it, you suddenly find yourself all alone. **No one is your friend any more.**

It's no fun to wind up with a little money and a lot of grief. **The next time you hear of a big lottery winner, remember that winners can be losers too.**

How to Keep a Teacher Happy

Keep Smiling
Act interested
Ask questions
 – during class
 – after class
Always have a good excuse when you don't do your homework
Laugh at teacher's jokes
Tell teacher how good he/she is looking
Use low voice to tell your friends the answers – so teachers can't hear
Always have pen or pencil
Write a lot in your notebook even if its only a note to your friend

Don't throw the board erasers around the room
Never, never say you're bored
Some teachers don't care about their students
Don't fall asleep in class
Don't change your seat every day so teacher has to look for you
Be polite to the school principal
Don't fly paper airplanes
Teachers have their own troubles
Don't get caught cutting
Don't keep asking to go to the bathroom

Trying It on Your Own

1. Here is the scribble sheet for a composition on "How to Keep a Teacher Happy." Look it over carefully. See what you can add. Then, do three things:

    a. Group the scribble sheet details.
    b. Write a unit paragraph based on the main idea that you develop from the scribble sheet.
    c. Expand your unit paragraph into a long composition with the same title— "How to Keep a Teacher Happy."

2. Okay, you're in the big time now! Below are three composition titles. Choose one of the titles and then take it every step of the way by yourself:

    a. Write out a scribble sheet and group your details.
    b. Develop your main idea and write a unit paragraph.
       (Don't forget to double-check the clue words in the titles.)
    c. Expand your unit paragraph into a composition that's four or five—or even six!—paragraphs long.

      I. Why Weekends Are Fun
     II. How to Be a Pest
    III. Problems of Going Steady

27
Writing Just for Fun

Here is a group of famous pictures by famous artists. Some of them may not look like any pictures you've ever seen before. Have fun with them anyhow! Write something about each one. Write as much or as little as you like. Write only a couple of sentences. Write four or five sensory words or action words that pop into your head as you look at a picture. Make up a scribble sheet or two. Tell a story. Write a description. Explain an idea or a feeling you get from a picture. Write one paragraph, or write four or five paragraphs.

Write anything! Just have a great time doing it!

Photo Credits

Grateful acknowledgment is given to the following sources: